AF608093

THE CATHOLIC UNIVERSITY OF AMERICA
CANON LAW STUDIES
No. 187

The Consecration and Blessing of Churches

A HISTORICAL SYNOPSIS AND COMMENTARY

BY

THADDEUS S. ZIOLKOWSKI, A.B., J.C.L.
Priest of the Diocese of St. Cloud

A DISSERTATION

Submitted to the Faculty of the School of Canon Law of the Catholic University of America in Partial Fulfillment of the Requirements for the Degree of Doctor of Canon Law

THE CATHOLIC UNIVERSITY OF AMERICA PRESS
WASHINGTON, D. C.
1943

Nihil Obstat:

Clemens V. Bastnagel, J.U.D.,
Censor Deputatus.

Washingtonii, D. C., die 6 maii 1943.

Imprimatur:

✠ Josephus F. Busch, D.D.,
Episcopus Sancti Clodoaldi.

Sti. Clodoaldi, Minnesota, die 19 maii 1943.

Printed by
The Paulist Press
New York, N. Y.
51

TO
HIS EXCELLENCY
THE MOST REVEREND JOSEPH F. BUSCH, D.D.
BISHOP OF ST. CLOUD
IN
REVERENCE AND GRATITUDE

TABLE OF CONTENTS

CHAPTER III

CHAPTER IV

CHAPTER V

PART TWO

THE CANONICAL COMMENTARY

FOREWORD

The custom of having certain places or buildings set apart from profane uses, and dedicated for a purely religious use, is as old as civilization itself.

The Israelites were directed to erect their Tabernacle when journeying across the desert, which was succeeded by Solomon's magnificent Temple at Jerusalem. Pagans of all times delighted in erecting magnificent temples in honor of their gods. The most primitive of heathen tribes consider as sacred their groves and grottos, where they assemble to perform their superstitious rites, and to pay homage to their idols. For Catholics, the church building has always been the center of all religious activity, especially since in the church building the Holy Sacrifice of the Mass, about which the Catholic faith centers, is celebrated. In the Catholic church building Christ lives and remains with us in the great Sacrament of the Most Holy Eucharist. Truly, the Catholic church building is the House of God. Hence, it is but natural that the early Christian writers testify to the existence of such special places of worship.

This dissertation is an attempt to bring about a clearer understanding of the sacredness of church buildings because of the act of ecclesiastical dedication, by which the church building becomes a sacred place, permanently withdrawn from profane uses, and a fitting place for the use of all faithful in their divine worship.

The present work is divided into two parts: an historical synopsis, and a canonical commentary. In the first part, the history and the evolution of canonical legislation dealing with the dedication of churches is traced from the early days of Christianity to the present Code of Canon Law. The second part contains the present Code legislation relative to the dedication of churches, with a commentary on the pertinent canons.

The writer takes this occasion to express his sentiments of genuine gratitude to the Most Rev. Joseph F. Busch, D.D., Bishop of St. Cloud, for the opportunity of graduate study in Canon Law; to the Rt. Rev. C. Thiebaut, Vicar General of the Diocese of St. Cloud, for has many kindnesses and his constant encouragement. The writer acknowledges also his deepest appreciation to the members of the Faculty of the School of Canon Law at the Catholic University of America for their direction and guidance in the preparation of this work; and to all who have in any way aided the writer in fulfilling his task for their courtesy and kindly interest.

Part One
Historical Synopsis

CHAPTER I

PRELIMINARY NOTIONS

The custom of having certain places set aside from profane uses, and of dedicating them for religious uses, is as old as civilization itself.

The present Code of Canon Law gives us a definition of what is meant by a *sacred place* in the canonical sense. "Sacred places are those which are set apart for divine worship, or for the burial of the faithful, by consecration or blessing, as prescribed by the approved liturgical books."[1] The term "divine worship" *(divina officia)* is defined in canon 2256, 1°.[2]

From canon 1154 it is evident that a place becomes sacred when it is set apart by acts which are called acts of consecration or of blessing. The purpose of the consecration or blessing is to withdraw the place from profane use, and to dedicate it to a religious use. Likewise profane acts are prohibited to be performed in sacred places. The violation or even desecration of a church follows if certain acts are committed therein, as enumerated in canon 1172. Furthermore, it is essential that the consecration or blessing be performed as prescribed by the approved liturgical books, since the Church alone gives to consecration or blessing the dedicatory efficacy of making

[1] Canon 1154. Translation by Woywod, S., *A Practical Commentary on the Code of Canon Law* (5. revised edition, 2 vols., New York: Wagner, 1939), 11, n. 1192.

[2] "Nomine divinorum officiorum intelliguntur functiones potestatis ordinis, quae de instituto Christi vel Ecclesiae ad divinum cultum ordinantur et a solis clericis fieri queunt."

a place sacred;[3] and hence the necessity, for the validity of the act, of using the form prescribed in the approved liturgical books.

The Code in canon 1165, § 1, repeats an ancient rule of law, namely, that divine services are not to be celebrated in a new church before it has been dedicated for divine worship.[4]

One must not confuse consecration with dedication, and blessing with dedication, or vice versa. "Dedication," in canon 1165, § 1, must be understood in a generic sense, that is, as a sacred action performed by a legitimate minister, by which with a definite formula of prayers, and a definite rite instituted by the Church, a place is set aside for a sacred use. The difference between consecration and blessing pertains solely to the ceremonies by which a church is dedicated. However, according to canon 1165, § 1,[5] the act of dedicating a church may be performed in a twofold manner, either by solemn consecration, or by simple blessing. The rite of consecration is found in the Roman Pontifical; the rite of blessing is found in the Roman Ritual.

The dedication of a church by solemn consecration essentially consists in anointing with chrism the twelve crosses which are placed on the walls or pillars of the church, with the formula: "Sanctificetur et consecretur hoc Templum in nomine Patris, et Filii, et Spiritus Sancti etc."[6]

[3] Wernz-Vidal, *Ius Canonicum* (7 vols. in 8, Romae: apud Aedes Universitatis Gregorianae, 1923-1938), IV, (*De Rebus*), pars I, n. 351; Vermeersch-Creusen, *Epitome Iuris Canonici* (3 vols., Vol. II, 6. ed., Mechliniae-Romae; Dessain, 1940), II, n. 470; Augustine, *A Commentary on the New Code of Canon Law* (8 vols., St. Louis: Herder, Vol. VI, 3. ed., *Administrative Law*, 1931), VI, 2; Ayrinhac, *Administrative Legislation in the New Code of Canon Law* (New York: Longmans, Green & Co., 1930), p. 2; Beste, *Introductio in Codicem* (Collegeville, Minnesota: St. John's Abbey Press, 1938), pp. 552-553; Coronata, *De Locis et Temporibus Sacris* (Taurini: Marietti, 1922), nn. 1-9; Grabowski, *Prawo Kanoniczne Wedlug Nowego Kodeksu* (Lwòw, Poland: Bibljoteka Religijna, 1927), pp. 474-483.

[4] Cc. 1, 11, 12, D. I, *de cons.*

[5] "Divina officia celebrari in nova ecclesia nequeunt, antequam eadem vel sollemni consecratione vel saltem benedictione divino cultui fuerit dedicata."

[6] S. R. C., 12 apr. 1614—*Decreta Authentica Congregationis Sacrorum Rituum ex Actis eiusdem collecta eiusque auctoritate promulgata sub auspiciis SS. D. N. Leonis Papae XIII* (6 vols., Romae: Ex Typographia Polyglotta—S. C. De Propaganda Fide, 1898-1927), n. 319. Hereafter cited *Decr. Auth.*

The dedication of a church by blessing essentially consists in sprinkling the upper and lower part of the walls, either inside or outside, with holy water, according to the formula in the Roman Ritual.[7]

At times the terms "Dedication" and "Consecration" were used indiscriminately.[8] Gasparri (1852-1934) [9] and Vermeersch (1858-1936)-Creusen [10] assert that the setting apart of a place for divine worship by solemn consecration is its dedication in the strict sense, since that was the only form of dedication used in the early days of the Church.[11] In a wider sense authors [12] refer to the dedication of a church as its consecration, since in the Roman Pontifical itself we find the title "De ecclesiae dedicatione seu consecratione." [13] The dedication of churches by solemn consecration will be discussed in the three following chapters: finally, in the last chapter of the historical summary, the dedication of churches by blessing.

The writer is concerned in this study solely with the dedication of churches. The word "church" will be used in its canonical sense as "a sacred building dedicated to divine worship, principally for the purpose that it may be used publicly, by all the faithful, for the exercise of divine worship." [14] For a detailed account of the

[7] S. R. C., 5 iun. 1899—*Decr. Auth.*, n. 4025.

[8] Devoti, *Institutionum Canonicarum Libri IV* (ed. 3., Gande, 1836), lib. II, tit. VII, sect. 1, par. XVIII, footnote (1).

[9] *Tractatus Canonicus de Sanctissima Eucharistia* (2 vols., Paris, 1897), I, n. 150.

[10] *Epitome Iuris Canonici,* II, n. 482.

[11] Cf. also Schmalzgrueber, *Ius Ecclesiasticum Universum* (5 vols. in 12, Romae, 1843-1845), lib. III, tit. XL, n. 4; Many, *Praelectiones De Locis Sacris* (Parisiis, 1904), n. 19.

[12] Reiffenstuel, *Ius Canonicum Universum* (5 vols. in 7, Parisiis, 1804-1882), lib. III, tit. 40, n. 2; Benedictus XIV, *De Sacrosancto Missae Sacrificio* (Editum a P. Josephus Schneider, Moguntiae: Sumptibus Francisci Kirchheim, 1879), lib. III, cap. VI, n. 1; De Angelis, *Praelectiones Iuris Canonici, ad Methodum Decretalium Gregorii IX Exactae* (4 vols. in 6, Romae: 1877-1887), lib. III, tit. 40, n. 2; Wernz-Vidal, *Ius Canonicum,* IV (Pars I), n. 360; Many, *De Locis Sacris,* nn. 17-18.

[13] *Pontificale Romanum Summorum Pontificum iussu editum a Benedicto XIV et Leone XIII Pontificibus Maximis recognitum et castigatum,* Ratisbonae: 1891.

[14] Canon 1161.

development in the various names which were applied to the early churches, the reader is referred to various authors who have furnished detailed expositions of the subjects.[15]

Lastly, in the preliminary section of this study an attempt will be made merely to indicate the historico-juridic development of the dedication of churches. It is entirely out of the scope of this study to probe into matters liturgical concerning the dedication of churches. At times it may be necessary to discuss and investigate early liturgical books, but this will be done only in so far as such investigations are necessary and helpful.

[15] Duchesne, *Christian Worship, Its Origin and Evolution* (Translated from the third French edition by M. L. McClure, London, 1903), pp. 399 ff.; Bingham, *The Antiquities of the Christian Church* (2 vols., London, 1856), bk. VIII, chap. I; Devoti, *Institutionum Canonicarum*, lib. II, tit. VII; Many, *De Locis Sacris*, n. 2; Wernz-Vidal, *Ius Canonicum*, Vol. IV, Pars I, nn. 352-353; Coronata, *De Locis Sacris*, nn. 11-12; Vermeersch-Creusen, *Epitome*, II, nn. 475-476; Beste, *Introductio in Codicem*, pp. 555-556; Ayrinhac, *Administrative Legislation*, nn. 5-6; Augustine, *Liturgical Law* (Herder, 1931), pp. 21-29.

CHAPTER II

DEDICATION OF CHURCHES IN THE EARLY PERIOD

Article 1. The First Three Centuries

The early Christians in the first three centuries undoubtedly had churches or places of worship. However, because of the fear of persecution the Christians refrained from exercising their acts of worship in public, which would attract the notice of the pagans, and would result in the confiscation of the building, and in death to the participants of the forbidden religion.[1]

The question of the Church's legal ability to hold property in the first three centuries is a very controversial subject, since the Church was not recognized as a legal organization by the Roman Law, and therefore could not hold any property in its *own name.* Charitable organizations, such as the *Collegia tenuiorum,* and burial associations, such as the *Collegia funeraticia,* were recognized by the Roman Law as having legal personality.[2] Because the Church performed such acts of mercy, legal protection could be granted to the property of the Christians.[3]

Many private and ordinary homes of the wealthier Christians were used for Christian worship, since they were very easily adapted for the divine worship of a Christian community.[4] Many times during the persecutions such property was confiscated, but then again ordered to be restored. Emperor Gallienus, in the year 260, revoked an edict of his predecessor Valerian (253-260) by ordering that all places dedicated to divine worship by the Christians be restored to them.[5]

[1] Devoti, *Institutionum Canonicarum Libri IV,* lib. II, tit. VII; Ferraris, s. v. "Ecclesia," art. I-IV.

[2] D. (47.22) 1; D. (3.4) 1.

[3] De Rossi, *Roma Sotteranea Christiana* (3 vols., Roma, 1864-1877), I, 101-103.

[4] Duchesne, *Christian Worship,* 399-400; Bingham, *The Antiquities of the Christian Church,* bk. 8, chap. I, sect. 13.

[5] Låemmer, *Eusebii Pamphili Historia Ecclesiastica* (Scaphusiae, 1862), p.

The famous Edict of Tolerance, given at Milan in the year 313 by Constantine and Licinius, finally gave religious freedom of worship to the Christians, with the proviso that any property of the Church which had been confiscated during the persecutions had to be restored.[6]

In this space of the first three centuries there is no definite document referring to the dedication of churches, or of the places used for worship. However, this is no direct indication for denying that there was some sort of dedication of places used for divine worship.

Burchard, Bishop of Worms (1002-1025), in his *Decretum* (circa 1095),[7] Ivo, Bishop of Chartres (1090-1117), in his *Panormia* (circa 1095),[8] and in his *Decretum* (circa 1090-1095),[9] quote Pope Felix IV (526-530),[10] and show that, because of the examples found in the Old Testament,[11] Christians consecrated their churches, as the Jews did their Temple, before using them for worship. Gratian incorporated this text into his *Decretum* (circa 1140),[12] showing the necessity of consecrating churches, and indicating that beyond the case of necessity Mass was not to be offered except in a church consecrated by a bishop.

Bingham (1668-1723)[13] does not admit the assertions of

546; Eusebius, *Historia Ecclesiastica,* VII, 13,—Migne, *Patrologiae Cursus Completus, Series Graeca* (161 vols., Parisiis, 1856-1866), XX, 674. Hereafter this title will be abbreviated *MPG.*

[6] Lactantius gives the full text of the decree, *De Mortibus Persecutorum,* XLVIII—Migne, *Patrologiae Cursus Completus, Series Latina* (221 vols., Parisiis, 1844-1864), VII, 267-270. Hereafter this title will be abbreviated *MPL.*

[7] Lib. III, cap. 57—*MPL,* CXL, 686.

[8] Lib. II, cap. 33—*MPL,* CLXI, 1085.

[9] Pars III, cap. 60—*MPL,* CLXI, 204.

[10] Jaffé, *Regesta Pontificum Romanorum ab Condita Ecclesia ad annum post Christum natum MCXCVIII* (2. ed., correctam et auctam auspiciis Gulielmi Wattenbach curaverunt S. Loewenfeld, F. Kaltenbrunner, P. Ewald, 2 vols. in 1. Lipsiae, 1885-1886), n. 878. Hereafter this work will be cited as Jaffé.

[11] Exodus, XXXI; Numbers, VII; Leviticus, VIII; 2 Kings, VII; 1 Paral., XXII; 2 Kings, XVI; 3 Kings, VIII.

[12] Cc. 1, 2, 11, 14, D. I, *de cons.*

[13] *The Antiquities of the Christian Church,* bk. VIII, chap. IX, sect. I.

Durantus (+1589),[14] or of Bona (+1674) [15] that the rite of consecration of churches is of Apostolic origin, because there aren't any authoritative documents or texts substantiating their assertions, as there are after the Edict of Milan (313).

It is probable that the early Christians had some form of dedicating their places of worship, but because of the persecutions the celebration could not be undertaken publicly, nor was the ceremonial as elaborate as it was after the year 313. This view is shared by many authors,[16] who do not admit a definite rite for the dedication of churches to have existed before the Edict of Tolerance, but do admit that some form of dedication for the places used for divine worship must have been employed even in the early days of the Church.[17]

Article 2. After the Edict of Milan (313)

A. *Definite Documents of Dedication*

Almost immediately after the persecution of Diocletian (284-305), during the reign of Constantine (306-337), there are definite documents of dedication of churches, which were then built in great numbers, and dedicated with great pomp and solemnity. Eusebius (+C. 339) writes: "After this there was brought about the spectacle for which we all prayed and longed: festivals of dedication in the cities and consecrations of the newly-built houses of prayer." [18] The

[14] "Ecclesias consecrandi consuetudo ab ipsis Apostolicis usque ad nostram manavit aetatem."—*De Ritibus Ecclesiae Catholicae Libri Tres* (Rome, 1591), lib. I, cap. XXIV, n. 1.

[15] "Templorum consecratione Veteri Testamento ad Novum, ab Apostolis ad Successores emanavit; atque hunc ritum servavit ecclesia totius Orientis et Occidentis consensu."—*De rebus liturgicis* (Romae, 1671), lib. I, cap. XX, n. 111.

[16] Bingham, *The Antiquities of the Christian Church,* bk. VIII, chap. IX, sect. I; Duchesne, *Christian Worship,* pp. 399-403; Wernz-Vidal, *Ius Canonicum,* IV, pars 1, n. 360, footnote 33; Many, *De Locis Sacris,* n. 10; Coronata, *De Locis et Temporibus Sacris,* n. 13; Augustine, *Liturgical Law,* p. 430.

[17] Cf. also Catalanus, *Pontificale Romanum* (3 vols., Parisiis, 1851), lib. II, tit. II, n. 1; Bliley, *Altars According to the New Code of Canon Law,* The Catholic University of America Canon Law Studies, n. 38 (Washington, D. C.: The Catholic University of America, 1927), pp. 31-32.

[18] *The Loeb Classical Library* (Edited by E. Capps; T. E. Page; W. H. D. Rouse),—Eusebius, *The Ecclesiastical History* (with an English Translation by

occasion was a very solemn one, because usually a great number of bishops were in attendance at the solemnity. Eusebius informs us of the splendid ceremony of the dedication of Constantine's Basilica at Tyre (314), which was dedicated in the presence of a large gathering of the clergy that came for the ceremony.[19] Socrates (+C. 450) observes that the Council of Antioch (341) was called purposely to dedicate the famous church there, called the ***Dominicum Aureum,*** which was begun by Constantine, and completed by Constantius (337-361). About 97 bishops are reported to have been present for the dedication of that church.[20]

The solemnity of dedication usually began with a panegyrical oration or sermon, which was in the nature of praise and thanksgiving to God for the building. At times also the founder was lauded, or the glory of the newly built church was extolled, as is evident from the flowery oration delivered by Eusebius (+C. 339) at the dedication of the Church of Paulinus (+329) at Tyre.[21]

At times more than one sermon was delivered, for Eusebius, writing of the dedication of churches in the time of Constantine, informs us that "Moreover, every one of the church's rulers that were present, according to his ability, delivered panegyrical orations, inspiring the assembly." [22] Some gave panegyrical orations upon the Emperor and the magnificence of his buildings; others adapted their sermons for the occasion; others discoursed on the lessons of Scripture that were read.[23]

When the sermons were delivered, then followed the unbloody Sacrifice offered to God; prayers were offered for the peace of the

Kirsopp Lake. In two volumes, New York: G. P. Putnam's Sons: 1926), II, p. 395. See also Laemmer, *Eusebii Pamphili Historia Ecclesiastica,* pp. 775-776; Eusebius, *Hist. Eccles.*, X, 3—*MPG,* XX, 847.

[19] Cf. Laemmer, *Eusebii Pamphili Historia Ecclesiastica,* pp. 776-811; Eusebius, *Hist. Eccles.,* X, 4—*MPG,* XX, 850.

[20] Socrates, *Historia Ecclesiastica,* III, 8—*MPG,* LXVII, 195. Cf. also Sozomenus, *Historia Ecclesiastica,* III, 5—*MPG,* LXVII, 1042.

[21] Laemmer, *Eusebii Pamphili Historia Ecclesiastica,* pp. 776-811; Eusebius, *Hist. Eccles.,* X, 4—*MPG,* XX, 850.

[22] *The Loeb Classical Library,* Eusebius, *The Ecclesiastical History,* II, p. 397; see also Laemmer, *Eusebii Pamphili Historia Ecclesiastica,* p. 776; *Hist. Eccles.,* X, 3—*MPG,* XX, 847.

[23] Eusebius, *De Vita Constantini,* IV, 43-46—*MPG,* XX, 1194.

world, for the prosperity of the Church, and for God's blessing on the Emperor and his subjects.[24]

B. *No Church to be Used Before Dedication*

A new church was not to be used as a place of worship before the dedication of the church took place, unless great necessity compelled the use of the building. This is evident from the apology that St. Athanasius (+373) made for himself to the Emperor Constantius (+361) when he used an unfinished church at Alexandria for the Easter services before it was dedicated.[25]

In the *Apology* St. Athanasius mentioned the fact that the multitude was very great, and the smaller churches could not accommodate the crowd without peril to their lives, and that therefore he was requested to permit the people to assemble in the great church, otherwise they threatened to meet in the open fields. Since this was a case of grave necessity, Athanasius permitted the services in the church. However, he told the Emperor that they still expected a day for the dedication of the church, when he should give the orders for its dedication, and then solemnly give his thanks to God for its completion, as was done in the time of his predecessor Alexander (+328). Churches at Trier and Aquileia were used because of urgent and grave necessities before they were completed, but their use for such a particular occasion was not their dedication.[26]

Synesius of Cyrene (+C. 415) relates a case in connection with which some contended that a certain place was consecrated as a church, because it had been used for prayers and the administration of the sacraments in time of a hostile invasion. Synesius positively determines that such a use of a place in time of necessity did not imply consecration, for otherwise mountains, valleys and private homes would be churches.[27]

[24] Laemmer, *Eusebii Pamphili Historia Ecclesiastica*, pp. 775-822; Eusebius, *Hist. Eccles.*, X, 3-5—*MPG*, XX, 845-879.

[25] Athanasius, *Apologia ad Imperatorem Constantium*, n. 14—*MPG*, XXV, 612.

[26] Athanasius, *loc. cit.*

[27] Synesius, *Epistola*, LXVII—*MPG*, LXVI, 1419.

C. *Bishops the Ordinary Ministers of Dedication*

The dedication of churches was generally performed with many bishops in attendance, hence they were the ministers employed in the dedicatory services. At times, however, it happened that none but the bishop of the diocese could attend, hence the obligation fell on the ordinary of the diocese to perform the dedication. This dedication by consecration was so specially reserved to the office of a bishop, that priests were not allowed to perform it under pain of deposition from office, as is evident from the I Council of Braga (561).[28]

An Irish Council under St. Patrick (C. 389—C. 461)[29] as early as the middle of the fifth century advised priests who were building a church not to offer Mass in it before the bishop consecrated it. If a priest did consecrate a church, there was no need of a new consecration, although the act was considered schismatical on the part of the priest, and was punished with deposition and degradation.[30]

Pope Gregory IX (1227-1241) condemned the custom of some bishops who delegated simple priests to reconcile consecrated churches.[31] This Pope asserted that the power of jurisdiction could be delegated, but what pertained to the power of episcopal orders

[28] C. XIX: "Item placuit, ut si quis presbyter, post hoc interdictum, ausus fuerit Chrisma benedicere, aut ecclesiam, aut altarium consecrare, a suo officio deponatur."—Hardouin, *Acta Conciliorum et Epistolae Decretales ac Constitutiones Summorum Pontificum* (12 vols., Parisiis, 1715), III, 352 (henceforth cited Hardouin); Mansi, *Sacrorum Conciliorum Nova et Amplissima Collectio* (53 vols. in 59, Paris Arnhem-Leipzig, 1901-1927), IX, 779 (hereafter cited Mansi).

[29] C. XXIII: "Si quis presbyterorum ecclesiam aedificaverit, non offerat, antequam adducat suum pontificem, ut eam consecret; quia sic decet."—Hardouin, I, 1792; Mansi, VI, 517.

[30] I Council of Braga (561), c. 19—Hardouin, III, 352; Mansi, IX, 779.

[31] "Aqua per episcopum benedicta ecclesiam reconciliari posse per alium episcopum non negamus; per sacerdotes hoc fieri de caetero prohibentes, non obstante consuetudine provinciae Bracharensis, quae dicenda est potius corruptela; quia, licet episcopus committere valeat quae iurisdictionis existunt, quae ordinis tamen episcopalis sunt, non potest inferioris gradus clericis demandare. Quod tamen mandantibus episcopis super reconciliatione factum est hactenus per eosdem, misericorditer toleramus."—c. 9, X, *de consecratione ecclesiae vel altaris,* III, 40.

could not be delegated to a simple priest. If a simple priest was not allowed to reconcile a consecrated church, *a fortiori* he was not allowed to consecrate a church. Since the Pope did not demand a reconciliation of such churches as were reconciled by a priest, the opinion is justified that the Pope validated the reconciliation which had been invalid from the beginning.[32]

Bishops were restricted to the consecration of churches in their own diocese. They could not consecrate a church in another diocese unless they were called to do so by the bishop of that diocese, or unless there was a vacancy of the bishopric. Bishops who transgressed this rule were suspended from offering Mass for a year.[33] Furthermore, even if a bishop built a church at his own expense in another diocese he could not assume the consecration personally, because the consecration of such a church was the right of the bishop in whose territory it was erected, and hence to consecrate the church, the bishop who had the church built needed permission from the bishop in whose diocese the church was located.[34]

The Emperor Justinian (527-565) [35] enacted that before anyone could build a church, the bishop was to be consulted, for the latter was to determine the place where the church could be built, and he was also to ascertain that the church was properly endowed and could be kept up once it was built. Furthermore, before the actual building was begun, the bishop was to be called to say solemn prayers and to make the sign of the cross on the place destined for the church.[36]

Theodosius II (408-450) [37] relates the custom which was ob-

[32] Cf. *glossa* in c. 9, X, *de consecratione ecclesiae vel altaris,* III, 40, v. "toleramus."

[33] III Council of Orleans (538), c. 15—Hardouin, II, 1426. See also Mansi, IX, 16; *Monumenta Germaniae Historica,* Legum Sectio III, *Concilia,* I (*Concilia Aevi Merovingici*), 78. (Recensuit Friedericus Maassen, Hannoverae, 1893); C. 7, q. 1, c. 28.

[34] I Council of Orange (441), c. 10—Hardouin, I, 1785; Mansi, VI, 437-438; Council of Chalcedon (451), c. 4, *Actio Decima Quinta*—Hardouin, II, 602-603; c. 9, D. I, *de cons.*

[35] N. (67.2).

[36] N. (131.7).

[37] C. Th. (16.10) 25.

served when the heathen temples were to be purified and consecrated into Christian churches, namely, that the temples were to be purified by placing in them the sign of the Christian religion, *i. e.*, the sign of the cross.

Article 3. Distinction in the Early Rite of Dedication

As to the rite of dedication it is essential to distinguish between the churches which possessed no relics, and hence were consecrated without relics, and churches which possessed relics, and hence were consecrated with relics. Authors [38] relate that there were two kinds of churches: first, the ordinary churches, which were merely meeting places for liturgical worship, such as the city churches or the country places of worship; secondly, the tombs of martyrs over which buildings of great size and magnificence were constructed, in order to shelter the assembly of the faithful who were desirous to hold liturgical services on the sites where the martyrs reposed and to honor their memory. If perchance the relics of the martyr were not there, then later they were transferred to their resting place with a solemn ceremonial if they were obtainable.[39]

Very shortly it came to be recognized that a martyr could have a number of tombs. Relics such as a piece of clothing saturated with the martyr's blood, or other objects which had been in close contact with the body of the martyr, especially those soaked in the martyr's blood, received an honor equal to that which was given to the body itself.[40] Churches with relics soon became as numerous

[38] Duchesne, *Christian Worship,* p. 402; Many, *De Locis Sacris,* n. 10; Augustine, *Liturgical Law,* p. 430.

[39] St. Ambrose (+397) mentions the translations of relics at the consecration of the basilica in Milan, in a letter written to his sister (386). Cf. *Epistola XXII,* I—*MPL,* XVI, 1019. Cf. also St. Jerome, *Contra Vigilantium,* 5—*MPL,* XXIII, 345; Theodoret, *Historia Ecclesiastica,* V, 36—*MPG,* LXXXII, 1206.

[40] Dooley, *Church Law on Sacred Relics,* The Catholic University of America Canon Law Studies, n. 70 (Washington, D. C.: The Catholic University of America, 1927), pp. 12-16; Schuster, *The Sacramentary* (5 vols., London: Burns, Oates and Washbourne, Ltd., 1924), I, 135; Many, *De Locis Sacris,* n. 110, nota I; Duchesne, *Christian Worship,* p. 402. Pontianus, a deacon, in his work *Acta Sancti Cypriani,* cap. 16—*MPL,* III, 1496, relates how the faithful spread towels and cloths around the body of St. Cyprian after his martyrdom, so as to save his blood which was shed for Christ.

as the rest, and eventually it was impossible to think of a church without relics in its altar.[41]

A. *Dedication of Churches Which Possessed no Relics*

After the year three hundred and thirteen bishops who consecrated a church used relics if these could be had. If relics were lacking, the consecrating bishop simply proceeded with the liturgical ceremony, since there was no legislation which required the presence of relics for the valid consecration of a church. In fact, Eusebius (+339) [42] and Sozomen (+C. 450),[43] in describing the rite of the dedication of churches, simply mention the gathering of the bishops, the solemn prayers with sermons or panegyrical orations delivered by the bishops, and finally the celebration of Mass.

Another evidence is the letter of Pope Vigilius (538-555) to Profuturus, Bishop of Braga, written about the year 538.[44]

B. *Dedication of Churches Which Possessed Relics*

When relics were had, the church was consecrated with them. The ceremony consisted in a solemn transferring of the relic to the church, and the placing of it in the altar (as in a tomb), which was equivalent to the interring of the body. The bishop blessed water

[41] Dooley, *loc. cit.*: Augustine, *Liturgical Law,* p. 431.

[42] *Hist. Eccles.,* X, 3-4; *De Vita Constantini,* IV, 43-45—*MPG,* XX, 845; 1194.

[43] *Hist. Eccles.,* II, 24—*MPG,* LXVII, 1007.

[44] *Epistola I,* n. 4: "Consecrationem cuiuslibet ecclesiae, in qua Spiritus Sancti ara non ponitur, celebritatem tantum scimus esse missarum. Et ideo, si qua sanctorum basilica a fundamentis etiam fuerit innovata, since aliquae dubitatione, cum in ea missarum fuerit celebrata solemnitas, totius sanctificatio consecrationis implebitur."—*MPL,* LXIX, 18. See also Hardouin, II, 1431-1432; Mansi, IX, 31-32; Hinschius, *Decretales Pseudo-Isidorianae et Capitula Angilramni* (Lipsiae, 1863), p. 711; Jaffé, n. 907: "Canon 83 Codicis Ecclesiae Africanae, qui canon ascribendus est concilio Carthaginensi (13 sept. 401), iubet quidem destrui memorias martyrum, 'in quibus nullum corpus aut reliquiae martyrum conditae probantur'; sed non vetat alias ecclesias aedificari sine reliquiis, ut legenti patet" (Bruns, *Concilia,* t. I, p. 176)—Many, *De Locis Sacris,* n. 110, p. 196, footnote 5. Part of the letter of Pope Vigilius was incorporated into the *Decretum* of Gratian, c. 24, D. I, *de cons.* Cf. *Braun, Der christliche Altar in seiner geschichtlichen Entwicklung* (2 vols., Munich, 1924), I, 540 for his evaluation of Canon 14 of the fifth Council of Carthage held in 401.

with chrism, mixed the mortar with the blessed water, and with this mixture sealed the altar stone containing the relics. After this followed the celebration of Holy Mass.[45]

This rite of dedication of churches is evident also from the letter of Pope Vigilius to Bishop Profuturus of Braga in 538, according to which with reference to the churches which had relics all that was required for consecration was the deposition of the relics and the celebration of Mass.[46]

In France at the beginning of the sixth century there is evidence of some rite having been instituted for the dedication of churches. A canon of the I Council of Orleans (511) [47] gave an instruction for the receiving of heretical clerics into the Catholic faith, and the consecration of their churches. What this order of consecration consisted of is difficult to ascertain.

Before the eighth century there was no general canonical legislation which commanded the dedication of churches with relics. In 787 the VII Ecumenical Council, the II of Nicaea, was the first to pass general legislation which required the consecration of churches with relics. It further decreed that all churches which had been consecrated without the relics of martyrs should have relics placed in them with the customary prayers. If a bishop was thenceforth found to consecrate a church without relics, he was to be deposed from office as a transgressor of ecclesiastical traditions.[48]

[45] The complete ceremonial is given by Duchesne, *Christian Worship*, pp. 399-418, pp. 478-479. Cf. also Bliley, *Altars*, pp. 30-42.

[46] *Epistola I—MPL*, LXIX, 18.

[47] C. 10: "De hereticis clericis, qui ad fidem Catholicam plena fide ac voluntate venerint, vel de basilicis quas in perversitate sua Gothi hactenus habueriunt, id censuimus observari: ut si clerici fideliter convertuntur, et fidem Catholicam integre confitentur, vel ita dignam vitam morum et actuum probitate custodiunt, officium, quo eos episcopus dignos esse consuevit, cum impositae manus benedictione suscipiant, et ecclesias simili, quo nostrae innovari solent, placuit ordine consecrari." *Monumenta Germaniae Historica*, Legum Sectio III, *Concilia*, I (*Concilia Aevi Merovingici*), 5 (Recensuit Friedericus Maassen, Hannoverae, 1893).

[48] C. 7: "Quaecunque templa consecrata sunt absque sancti reliquiis martyrum, definimus in eis reliquiarum una cum solita oratione fieri positionem. Et si a praesenti tempore fuerit episcopus absque lipsanis consecrare templum, deponatur, ut ille qui ecclesiasticas traditiones transgreditur."—Hardouin, IV,

Twenty-nine years later, at the Synod of Chelsea in England (816), bishops were commanded to consecrate the churches built in their diocese by blessing water for the ceremony, and by using the rite as found in the liturgical books. The Eucharist consecrated by the bishop was to be placed in a receptacle with other relics, and preserved in the church. If relics could not be had, it was sufficient that the Eucharist be used, because it was the Body and Blood of Our Lord, Jesus Christ.[49]

The *Liber Diurnus Romanorum Pontificum,* which consisted of a compilation of formularies used from the fifth to the eleventh century by the Apostolic Chancery for the execution of documents, and which therefore contains the practice and customs of the Roman Curia, reports a petition concerning the dedication of an oratory. The reply was that the dedication was to proceed with the customary blessing *(solita benedictione).*[50] Here the mere mention is made that the customary blessing *(solita benedictio)* is to be used, but no description of the rite is given. A short description of the more important liturgical books will be helpful to determine the rite of dedication of churches in the various centuries.

491; Mansi, XIII, 751; cf. Schroeder, *Disciplinary Decrees of the General Councils* (St. Louis: Herder, 1937), p. 148.

[49] Synod of Chelsea (816), c. 10—Hardouin, IV, 1220; cf. also Duchesne, *Christian Worship,* p. 403, footnote 1.

[50] *Liber Diurnus,* ed. Garnier—*MPL,* CV, 92; De Rozière, *Liber Diurnus ou Recueil des Formules usitées par la Chancellerie Pontificale du Ve au Xie* siècle (Paris, 1869), nn. X-XI, pp. 36-40. "The *Liber Diurnus* contains three series of formulas; the old (formulas 1-63), collected in the time of Pope Honorius I (circa 625); the second (formulas 64-81), collected (circa 670); the third (formulas 82-99), collected during the time of Pope Adrian (772-795)—Cicognani, *Canon Law* (2. ed., Philadelphia: Dolphin Press, 1935), p. 231, and Van Hove, *Commentarium Lovaniense,* Vol. I, Tom. I, *Prolegomena ad Codicem Iuris Canonice* (Mechliniae: H. Dessain, 1928), n. 142. W. Peitz (*Liber Diurnus, Beiträge zur Kenntnis der ältesten päpstlichen Kanzlei vor Gregor dem Grossen,"* in *Sitzungsberichte der Akademie der Wiss,* Tom. 185, Vienna, 1918) contends that the old series of formulas and part of the second series were compiled already before the time of Pope Gregory the Great (590-604). M. Tangl (*Gregors Register und Liber diurnus,* in *Neues Archiv,* XLI [1917-1919], 741-752) disagrees. Cf. Van Hove, *Prolegomena,* n. 142, footnote 4. For a review of recent opinions on the *Liber Diurnus* see Leo Santifaller, "Zum Liber Diurnus —Forschung,"—*Historische Zeitschrift,* CLXI (1940), 532-538.

CHAPTER III

DEDICATION OF CHURCHES IN THE ROMAN LITURGICAL BOOKS

In the Latin Church from the fifth and sixth centuries liturgical books were compiled, by which the rite and practice to be observed in liturgical functions were stabilized. In the Greek Church these liturgical books were called *Euchologia,* (glory, honor); in the Latin Church they were called: *Libri Mysteriorum, Libri Sacramentorum,* and *Sacramentaria.*[1]

The origin of our present day Missal, Pontifical, Ritual, and Gradual may be traced to the Leonine Sacramentary,[2] the Gelasian Sacramentary,[3] the Gregorian Sacramentary,[4] the *Ordines Romani*[5] and the *Liber Responsalis sive Antiphonarius.*[6]

There are extant other ancient manuscripts of Sacramentaries besides those mentioned above, namely, the *Missale Gothicum,* the *Missale Gallicanum,* the *Vetus Missale Francorum* and the *Ambrosian Books,* compiled for churches using the Ambrosian Rite, and many others, which need not be mentioned here.[7] Worthy of our attention are the Leonine, the Gelasian and the Gregorian Sacramentaries, and also the Roman Ordinals.

[1] Van Hove, *Prolegomena,* nn. 137-139; Cicognani, *Canon Law,* p. 230; Duchesne, *Christian Worship,* pp. 64-74; pp. 120-160.

[2] Found in *MPL,* LV, 21 ff.; see also Feltoe, *Sacramentarium Leonianum* (Cambridge, 1896).

[3] Text in *MPL,* LXXIV, 1049; Muratori, *Liturgia Romana Vetus,* I, 36; see also Wilson, *The Gelasian Sacramentary* (Oxford: 1894).

[4] Text in *MPL,* LXXVIII, 25; Muratori, *Liturgia Romana Vetus,* I, 10; see also Wilson, *The Gregorian Sacramentary* (London: 1915).

[5] Text in *MPL,* LXXVIII, 937; Muratori, *Liturgia Romana Vetus,* II, 469.

[6] Text in *MPL,* LXXVIII, 641.

[7] Cf. Van Hove, *Prolegomena,* nn. 137-139; Duchesne, *Christian Worship,* chapters II and V; Cicognani, *Canon Law,* 230-233; Beste, *Introductio in Codicem,* 21.

Article 1. The Leonine Sacramentary

The Leonine Sacramentary gives the liturgical formulas as used in Rome from the time of Pope St. Damasus I (366-384) to the time of Pope St. Leo I (440-461). It was falsely attributed to the latter pope [8] because the liturgical formulas correspond in style to Pope Leo's epoch. The more common opinion [9] is that the Leonine Sacramentary is a private and personal collection of the middle or of the end of the sixth century, compiled by a scribe who had at his command the liturgical books used in Rome at the various basilicas, and drawn from the best sources of his time. Episcopal functions and formulas are described. The list of functions is very impressive: Mass for the Dedication of Churches; the Consecration of Bishops; the Ordination of Deacons and Priests; the Consecration of Virgins; the Solemn Blessing of Spouses and the *Velatio Nuptialis*. The very significant Consecration Prefaces of our present Pontifical, which are so rich in literary beauty, are found in this sacramentary.[10]

The Leonine Sacramentary only lists the Mass for the Dedication of Churches. One must not confuse this Mass with the dedicatory rite itself, for the Holy Sacrifice usually followed the ceremonies of dedication.[11]

Article 2. The Gelasian Sacramentary

There is a controversy as to the origin of this Sacramentary. It is of no purpose here to study this controversy; hence the reader may simply be referred to the authors.[12] The Sacramentary is attributed to Pope St. Gelasius I (492-496). On the testimony of Walafried Strabo (+849)[13] Pope Gelasius had a share in the com-

[8] Van Hove, *Prolegomena*, n. 139; Cicognani, *Canon Law*, 230; De Puniet, *The Roman Pontifical* (Longmans, Green & Co., 1932), p. 11.

[9] Van Hove, *loc. cit.*; Cicognani, *loc. cit.*; De Puniet, *loc. cit.*; Duchesne. *Christian Worship*, pp. 135-144.

[10] De Puniet, *Roman Pontifical*, p. 11.

[11] Duchesne, *Christian Worship*, p. 403, footnote 2.

[12] Cf. Van Hove, *Prolegomena*, n. 139; Duchesne, *Christian Worship*, pp. 125-134; Cicognani, *Canon Law*, 231; De Puniet, *The Roman Pontifical*, pp. 12-17; Ziegler, "Pope Gelasius I and His Teaching on the Relation of Church and State," *The Catholic Historical Review*, XXVII (1942), 415-418.

[13] *Libellus De exordiis et incrementis quarundam in observationibus ecclesiasticis rerum.*; Cf. *MGH*, Leges, Sectio II (*Capitularia*), II, 471-516.

pilation of the Roman Sacramentary. The prayers collected by this Pope were still in use in the Churches of Gaul in Strabo's own day. Many churches desired to conform to the Roman custom, but St. Gregory the Great, struck with the imperfection of Gelasius' book, revised it and made of it the Gregorian *Liber Sacramentorum.*

Fifty years after Walafried Strabo's death, at the end of the ninth century, John the Deacon, the biographer of St. Gregory the Great (590-604), wrote: "Sed et Gelasianum codicem de Missarum solemniis multa subtrahens, pauca convertens, nonnulla vera superadiciens pro exponendis evangelicis lectionibus solemniis, . . . in unius libri volumine coarctavit." [14]

These two testimonies are from the ninth century, when it was believed that a Sacramentary of Gelasius existed, and that the Gregorian Sacramentary was merely a revision of the Gelasian Sacramentary.

In regard to the dedication of churches, the latter Sacramentary contains the following: a beautiful oration invoking God's blessing on all who prayed in the church; an oration said over the wine mixed with water which was to be used for the consecration of the altar; orations for the consecration of the altar; an oration also for the consecration of the sacred vessels, such as the chalice and the paten, and for the blessing of the linens. These orations are listed and grouped together in view of their connection and use in the church. Finally, there was a list of orations which were to be used in the Mass of Dedication.[15] There is no evidence of a permanent or fixed dedicatory rite to be found at this time.

Article 3. The Gregorian Sacramentary

The Gregorian Sacramentary was compiled by Pope St. Gregory the Great (590-604), as is evident from the testimony of John the Deacon, the biographer of St. Gregory.[16]

[14] *Vita S. Greg.*, II, 17—*MPL,* LXXV, 94.

[15] *Sacramentarium Gelasianum—MPL,* LXXIV, 1138-1142; Muratori, *Liturgia Romana Vetus,* I, 609-614; Wilson, *The Gelasian Sacramentary* (Oxford: 1894).

[16] *Vita S. Greg.*, II, 17—*MPL,* LXXV, 94.

Pope Adrian I (772-795) in a letter to Charlemagne, written between 784 and 791, indicated that the King had asked that the Sacramentary compiled by St. Gregory be sent to him from Rome, and then stated that it was sent to Charlemagne by John, a monk and the Abbot of a monastery at Ravenna.[17]

The original text of the Gregorian Sacramentary was supplemented by Alcuin (+804) between 794-800, according to testimony by Bernaldus of Constance (+1100).[18] In the use of this Sacramentary it is necessary to distinguish carefully between the Gregorian text which represents the pure Roman use at the end of the eighth century, on the one hand, and the supplement, on the other.[19] During the ninth and tenth centuries additions were made and the distinction between the original text and the supplement was no longer maintained. The title of "Gregorian" was now used to designate the whole Sacramentary.[20]

The Gregorian Sacramentary contains the following ceremonies for the dedication of a church: the entrance of the bishop with introductory prayers, the ceremony of the alphabet, the preparation of the lustral water, the lustration of the altar, the lustration of the walls of the church, the consecration of the altar with holy oil, the deposition of relics of the saints in the altar, the anointing of the walls of the church in twelve places, and the offering of the Mass of Dedication. These ceremonies, as may be noticed, are similar in great part to those found in the present Roman Pontifical.[21]

Article 4. Roman Ordinals

Along with the Sacramentaries of the Roman Church there came into being other documents which exerted a great influence on our present liturgical books, namely the *Ordines Romani*. In the Roman Ordinals one finds the order of the ceremonies for which the Sacramentaries give only the words, and hence the information which they give is very valuable. The early Ordinals describe only the ceremonies

[17] Jaffé, n. 2473; Mansi, XII, 796.

[18] *Micologus de Ecclesiasticis Observationibus,* LX—*MPL,* CLI, 1020.

[19] De Puniet, *The Roman Pontifical,* p. 23.

[20] De Puniet, *loc. cit.*

[21] *Pontificale Romanum,* tit. *De Ecclesiae Dedicatione seu Consecratione.*

performed by the pope. Nevertheless, it was not long until they were used as models for the pontifical functions celebrated by the bishops, and they were known currently with the Sacramentaries in France, Germany, and England.[22]

The Ordinals regulated the ceremonial of the Mass, of baptism, of ordinations, of the dedication of churches, and of other solemn functions. These *Ordines* at first existed in the form of single booklets, according to the testimony of Amalarius of the ninth century: "ut ex scripturis discimus quae continent per diversos libellos Ordinem Romanum." [23]

From the beginning of the ninth century and increasingly in the tenth, the trend was more and more to group the *Ordines* together into collections. Eventually they were placed alongside of the formulas of the Sacramentaries and were thus absorbed by the latter. Not all of these *Ordines* were of the same date. Traces of changes in the Pontifical liturgy from the ninth to the fifteenth centuries may been detected in them.[24]

The Roman Sacramentaries and Ordinals were copied and recopied outside the city of Rome, and supplements were frequently added. In regard to the dedication of churches one may safely assume that the dedicatory rite was not uniform in the Universal Church. For the purpose of noting the evolution in the ceremonies of the dedication of churches, one may turn to the works of the following important writers: to Egbert, Archbishop of York (+766);[25] to Walafried Strabo (+849);[26] to Rhabanus Maurus (+856);[27] St.

[22] Muratori, *Liturgia Romana Vetus,* II, 469; Duchesne, *Christian Worship,* p. 150; Cicognani, *Canon Law,* p. 231; Mabillon, *Museum Italicum,* 2 vols., Paris, 1687-1689. Cf. also *MPL,* LXXVIII, 937-1372.

[23] *De Ordine Antiphonarii,* LII—*MPL,* CV, 1295.

[24] Sixteen *Ordines* are listed in *MPL,* LXXVIII, 937-1372; Muratori, *Liturgia Romana Vetus,* II, 469.

[25] *Excerptiones Egberti* (747)—*MPL,* LXXXIX, 379-400. Many of the decrees of Egbert were incorporated into the *Decretum* (*MPL,* CXL, 537-1058), of Burchard of Worms (+1025); the *Decretum* (*MPL,* CLXI, 47-1037), and *Panormia* (*MPL,* CLXI, 1038-1344), of Ivo of Chartres (+1117); and the *Decretum* of Gratian (+ before 1158).

[26] *Libellus de exordiis et incrementis quarundam in observationibus ecclesiasticis rerum—MGH,* Leges, Sectio II (*Capitularia*), II, 471-516.

[27] *De Clericorum Institutione,* II, 45—*MPL,* CVII, 293-419.

Peter Damien (+1072);[28] Hugo of St. Victor (+1140);[29] and Sicardus of Cremona (+1215).[30]

At the end of the eleventh century one finds practically all the ceremonies described, as they are prescribed today in the Roman Pontifical of the Dedication of Churches.

28 *Sermones LXIX-LXXII, In Dedicatione Ecclesiae—MPL,* CXLIV, 897-912.

29 *De Sacramentis,* lib. II, pars V, cap. 11—*MPL,* CLXXVI.

30 *Mitrale, I,* 6-10—*MPL,* CCXIII, 28-36.

CHAPTER IV

THE ROMAN PONTIFICAL AND THE DEDICATION OF CHURCHES

ARTICLE 1. THE PONTIFICAL TO THE COUNCIL OF TRENT

IN regard to the compilation of a Pontifical, attempts were made in earlier times, but not with complete success. Worthy of mention in this connection are *The Excerpts of Egbert* (747), Archbishop of York (+766).[1]

At the end of the thirteenth century a Pontifical was drawn up by William Durantis (+1296), a canonist of note at the Roman Curia and later Bishop of Mende (1285-1296). This Pontifical was submitted to the Latin bishops for their acceptance, and it was destined to play a decisive part in the formation of the present Pontifical.[2]

An official edition of the Pontifical appeared in 1485 under the editorship of John Burchard (+1506), later Bishop of Civita Castellana and Orte (1503-1506), and of Bishop Augustine Patrizi of Pienza (+1490), known also as Piccolomini, because he had been adopted by Aeneas Silvius Piccolomini, the future Pope Pius II (1458-1464), whose secretary he was.[3] In the preface to the Pontifical of 1485, which Piccolomini addressed to Pope Innocent VIII (1484-1492), it is evident that Innocent VIII had given official instructions to revise the text of the Pontifical and reprepare an edition that was to be submitted as authentic to all the bishops of the Latin world.[4]

Every diocese had its particular usages. There were also dis-

[1] *Excerptiones Egberti—MPL,* LXXXIX, 379-400.

[2] De Puniet, *The Roman Pontifical,* pp. 37-42.

[3] De Puniet, *The Roman Pontifical,* pp. 44-49; Van Hove, *Prolegomena,* n. 242.

[4] "Sanctissimo in Christo patri et domino nostro Innocentio . . . papae VIII . . . Pontificalis libri emendationem B. P. tuo iussu aggressus sum; opus sane laboriosum varium. . . ." This text is quoted in De Puniet, *The Roman Pontifical,* pp. 56-57.

crepancies between different copies of the Pontifical. Since errors crept into reprints, a new corrected edition was published at Rome in 1497 during the Pontificate of Alexander VI (1492-1503). In 1511 a new edition of Piccolomini's Pontifical was published in Venice and Lyons. This edition is known as the Pontifical of Julius II (1503-1513). In 1520 the Dominican Albert Castellani (+1522) dedicated a revised edition to Pope Leo X (1513-1521) but even this edition was not without errors.[5]

Article 2. The Council of Trent, Clement VIII, and the First Official Publication of the *Pontificale Romanum* (1595)

At the end of the sixteenth century the Roman Church had an authentic Pontifical for the use of bishops. By order of the Roman Pontiffs the Pontifical was revised more than once. The popes did not invest the Pontifical with their formal approval, nor did the popes impose the various editions of the Pontifical upon the bishops to be used exclusively by them in pontifical functions. Hence in regard to the Dedication of Churches, whatever Sacramentary or Pontifical a bishop had, that was the one that was used, so that no doubt ceremonies differed in different dioceses.

Pope Sixtus V on January 22, 1588, in his Constitution *"Immensa"* established a number of Roman Congregations, of which the fifth was the *Congregatio pro sacris ritibus et caeremoniis,*[6] consisting of five cardinals to whom was entrusted the duty of correcting the liturgical books.[7]

The project of Sixtus V (1585-1590) was revived by Clement VIII (1592-1605). As a basis for the reform of the existing Pontifical, Clement VIII took Castellani's edition of 1520. Corrections were made and the new book which was published in 1595 had the

[5] An addition which impaired the validity of Ordinations is noted by Benedict XIV (*De Synodo Diocesana,* lib. VIII, C. XI). This addition does not appear in the editions of the Pontifical of Clement VIII (1592-1605) and Urban VIII (1623-1644); De Puniet, *The Roman Pontifical,* pp. 47-53.

[6] *Bullarium Diplomatum et Privilegiorum Romanorum Pontificum Taurinensis Editio* (25 vols., Augustae Taurinorum, 1857-1872), VIII, 989. Hereafter this work will be quoted as *Bullarium Romanum.*

[7] *Bullarium Romanum,* VIII, 989-990.

official title of *Pontificale Romanum.* A year later, on February 10, 1596, Clement VIII in his Constitution *"Ex quo in Ecclesia Dei"* [8] officially promulgated the *Pontificale Romanum* as the exclusive book for all Pontifical functions in the Western Church. From that date all private Pontificals, whether approved or not, were suppressed, and it was made obligatory to replace them with the official *Pontificale Romanum.* From that time on there was established an authoritative, uniform, and set Rite to be used exclusively by all Latin bishops in the dedication of churches through consecration.

Article 3. The Roman Pontifical from 1595 to the Code

Revisions were made in the Roman Pontifical by Pope Urban VIII (1623-1644) and the revised edition was published in 1645. Pope Benedict XIV in 1752 made several additions, and Pope Leo XIII in 1888 reissued the Roman Pontifical. The latest typical edition appeared in Rome in 1934.[9] At present the Code in canon 1257 asserts the right of the Holy See alone to regulate the sacred liturgy, and to approve liturgical books.[10]

The first or typical edition of a liturgical book may be printed only by either the Papal *Typographia Polyglotta* at the Vatican, or by one of the printers accredited by the Holy See. The necessary permission must be obtained from the Sacred Congregation of Rites.[11] The details of printing a *typical* edition are outlined in a decree of the Sacred Congregation of Rites, May 17, 1911.[12] Once the typical edition has been completed, any printer may with the approval of the local Ordinary reprint the liturgical books, on condition that the original edition is followed, and that the local Ordinary attests that the texts as published agree with the approved editions.[13]

[8] *Bullarium Romanum,* X, 246—*Fontes,* n. 180.

[9] Dausend, "Pontificale Romanum"—*Lexikon Für Theologie Und Kirche,* VIII, pp. 372-373.

[10] Canon 1257: Unius Apostolicae Sedis est tum sacram ordinare liturgiam, tum liturgicos approbare libros.

[11] Clemens VIII, const. *"Cum in Ecclesia,"* 10 maii, 1602—*Bullarium Romanum,* X, 788. Cf. canon 1399, n. 10.

[12] *AAS,* III (1911), 242.

[13] Canon 1390.

CHAPTER V

DEDICATION OF CHURCHES BY BLESSING

ARTICLE 1. EVIDENCE OF DEDICATION OF CHURCHES BY BLESSING

THE present Code in canon 1165, § 1, repeats an ancient rule of law [1] that Holy Mass and other divine services may not be celebrated in a new church until it has been dedicated to divine worship. This dedication of a church to divine worship according to the present law may be effected either by a solemn consecration or by a blessing.[2]

The Code does not absolutely insist on the consecration of all churches, but demands only the blessing of some churches before they are to be used for divine worship. There is, however, a strong appeal in the Code that cathedral churches should be dedicated by solemn consecration, and also, in so far as it is possible, collegiate, conventual and parochial churches.[3]

The rite of dedicating a church by consecration was very simple after the Edict of Milan in 313, and the elaborate rite as it exists in the present Roman Pontifical reached its present form with the diffusion of the Sacramentaries.[4]

To determine the exact time when the dedication of churches by a simpler form of blessing was first introduced into the Church is very difficult. The earliest positive canonical legislation may be determined indirectly from two decretals of Pope Gregory IX (1227-1241). In the one decretal Pope Gregory IX wrote:

> "Si ecclesia *non consecrata* [italics not in the original] cuiuscunque semine fuerit aut sanguinis effusione polluta, aqua protinus exorcizata lavetur, ne divinae laudis in ea organa suspendantur; est tamen, quam citius fieri poterit consecranda." [5]

[1] C. 3, 11, 12, D. I., *de cons.*

[2] Canon 1165, § 1: "Divina officia celebrari in nova ecclesia nequeunt, antequam eadem vel sollemi consecratione vel saltem benedictione divino cultui fuerit dedicata."

[3] Canon 1165, § 3: "Sollemni consecratione dedicentur ecclesiae cathedrales et, quantum fieri potest, ecclesiae collegiatae, conventuales, paroeciales."

[4] Cf. Chap. III of this work.

[5] C. 10, X, *de consecratione ecclesiae vel altaris,* III, 40.

In the other decretal Gregory IX wrote:

> "Ecclesiae, in qua divina mysteria celebrantur, *licet adhuc non exstiterit consecrata,* [italics not in the original] nullo iure privilegium immunitatis adimitur: quia obsequiis divinis dedicata nullius est temerariis ausibus profananda." [6]

From these two decretals it is evident that there were during the time of Gregory IX churches which were not consecrated, but were nevertheless used for divine worship. On the other hand, there is no express mention of dedication by blessing. According to the second decretal mentioned above,[7] even a non-consecrated church in which Mass was offered enjoyed immunity, for it was dedicated by the holding of divine services in it.

Gulczynski makes an observation which is important to be considered:[8]

> "The violation of a church is synonymous with the pollution of a church. Both terms were used interchangeably throughout the history of the development of Canon Law. The terms were already in use before the time of the Decretals of Gregory IX, but in this earlier period the violation or pollution of a church caused the church to become desecrated, that is, it lost its consecration. With the great development of the science of Canon Law in the twelfth and thirteenth centuries, the term 'violation of a church' lost its former meaning. The Decretals of Gregory IX no longer considered the violation of a church as a loss of consecration. From this time forward the violation of a church was considered a moral contamination of the sanctity of the church which occurred as a result of certain acts committed within the church. The moral contamination continued to exist until the pristine sanctity of the church was restored by the rite of reconciliation."

How was a church made to possess this sanctity? Three possibilities are suggested: (1) the dedication of the church by solemn consecration; (2) the celebration of Mass in a non-consecrated

[6] C. 9, X, *De immunitate ecclesiarum, coemiterii, et rerum ad eas pertinentium,* III, 49.

[7] C. 9, X, *De immunitate ecclesiarum, coemiterii, et rerum ad eas pertinentium,* III, 49.

[8] *The Desecration and Violation of Churches,* The Catholic University of America Canon Law Studies, n. 159 (Washington, D. C.: The Catholic University of America Press, 1942), pp. 30-31.

church; (3) the dedication of a church by a simple blessing. This simple blessing, which no doubt at first was a temporary substitute for consecration, gradually grew into a custom, so that it was sufficient to have a church dedicated with this simple blessing. The power to bless churches could be delegated by a bishop to a priest.[9]

It is impossible to determine definitely the year in which the distinction between blessing and consecration was introduced. Most of the authors pass over that issue. With certainty one can only know that it was before the time of the promulgation of the Decretals of Gregory IX in 1234.

Catalanus (+ after 1757) [10] in his commentary on the Roman Ritual places the year 1000 as the time when churches had to be at least blessed, if they were not already consecrated, before the Holy Sacrifice of the Mass could be offered in them.

De Bonis (+ after 1761) [11] openly asserts that it is not clear in what century the distinction between blessing and consecration was introduced. He does not deny the possibility that the distinction was introduced at the time when the number of churches grew to such proportions that it was impossible for the bishops to attend to the consecration of all of the churches. While consecration was an act of the episcopal order and could not be delegated to a priest, yet the simple blessing, although in itself as a function of the priestly order it was an act of jurisdiction reserved to bishops, could be delegated by the bishops to a priest. The whole question is hidden in obscurity, since it is difficult to determine the century in which churches grew in number to such proportions that it was impossible for bishops to attend to the consecration of all of them. At most one can say that the blessing of a church was a canonical institute which had gradually come into existence in the Church some time before the pontificate of Gregory IX.

Immediately after the Decretals of Gregory IX very important

[9] Many, *De locis sacris,* n. 10; Ayrinhac, *Administrative Legislation,* n. 12.

[10] *Rituale Romanum Benedicti Papae XIV, Perpetuis Commentariis Exornatum ac in duos Tomos divisum* (Patavii, 1760), Tomus II, Titulus VIII, Cap. XXIX, n. VIII.

[11] *De Oratoriis Publicis* (Mediolani, 1761), cap. X, n. 164.

legislation is to be found in the Council of London (1237).[12] This Council deplored the fact that because of negligence even cathedral churches used for divine worship were not consecrated. Therefore the Council enjoined the obligation on all bishops to have all cathedral, conventual, and parochial churches, if they had strong walls, consecrated within two years, those already in existence and those that would be built in the future. If a bishop was impeded, then he was to give authority to another bishop to perform the consecration; otherwise the use of the church remained interdicted up to the moment that it was consecrated.

There is no direct legislation in the Council of Trent (1545-1563) on the dedication of churches, either by consecration or by blessing. Reference is made to the dedication of churches in a decree concerning the things that are to be observed and avoided in the celebration of Mass, when the Council repeated the ancient legislation [13] that seculars and regulars were not to celebrate the Sacrifice of Holy Mass in private homes or entirely outside of a church or an oratory dedicated solely to divine worship.[14]

Article 2. Dedication by Blessing and the Roman Ritual

As in the circumstance of the dedication of a church by consecration, so also in regard to the dedication of a church by blessing, no authoritative general legislation was indicated for observance in the dedicatory rite until the official promulgation of the Roman Ritual which took place by order of Pope Paul V in 1614.

The Council of Trent did not forbid the use of other Rituals which existed at the time. It merely defined that the received and approved rites of the Catholic Church could not be contemned or omitted without sin, or set at naught by her ministers, and that they could not be changed by any pastor.[15]

[12] Canon 1—Mansi, XXIII, 447-448; Hardouin, VII, 292-293.

[13] Canon 12, 33, 34; D. I., *de econs.*

[14] Conc. Trident., sess. XXII, *de observandis et evitandis in celebratione missae;* Schroeder, *Canons and Decrees of the Council of Trent* (St. Louis: Herder Book Co., 1941), p. 150.

[15] Conc. Trident., sess. VII, *de Sacramentis,* canon 13; Schroeder, *Canons and Decrees of the Council of Trent,* p. 53.

The Roman Ritual was based on the *Sacerdotale Romanum.* The latter was compiled by the Dominican Castellani, was first printed in 1537, and later revised by F. Samarino and published in 1579.[16]

On June 17, 1614, Paul V (1605-1621) by his Constitution *"Apostolicae Sedi"* promulgated and issued an official edition of the Roman Ritual. Therein he appealed to all bishops, abbots, and pastors to use the authentic Roman Ritual in the sacred functions and to keep the traditional rites intact. There was a dispute whether the Roman Ritual was obligatory for the whole Church. It arose in view of the term used by Paul V in his Constitution of promulgation in which the Pontiff wrote:

> "*hortamur,* in Domino Venerabiles Fratres Patriarchas, Archiepiscopos, Episcopos, et dilectos filios eorum Vicarios, necnon Abbates, Parochos universos, ubique locorum existentes, et alios at quos spectat, ut in posterum tamquam Ecclesiae Romanae filii eiusdem Ecclesiae omnium Matris, et Magistrae auctoritate constituto Rituali in sacris functionibus utantur, et in re tanti momenti, quae Catholica Ecclesia, et ab ea probatus usus antiquitatis statuit; inviolate observent." [17]

The terms used by Pius V and Clement VIII in the promulgation of the Pontifical were much stricter, and therefore the Roman Ritual was not considered previously to their time to be of strict obligation for all alike in the whole Church. Catalanus [18] in the preface to the Roman Ritual edited by Benedict XIV admitted the use of other rituals besides the Roman Ritual edited by Paul V in 1614. Bouix (1808-1870) [19] refuted the opinion of Catalanus by proposing arguments to show that the Roman Ritual of Paul V was obligatory for the whole Church, and had to be followed by all Latin bishops in preference to any other existing ritual.

[16] Thalhofer, *Handbuch der katholischen Liturgik* (2 vols., Freiburg, 1883-1890), I, 46; Zaccaria, *Bibliotheca Ritualis* (2 vols. in 3, Romae, 1776-1781), I, pp. 137-144.

[17] Paulus V, const. *"Apostolicae Sedi,"* 17 iun. 1614, § 4; *Fontes,* n. 198.

[18] *Benedicti XIV Rituale Romanum,* Prefatio.

[19] *Institutiones Juris Canonici, Tractatus de Jure Liturgico* (Parisiis, 1860), pp. 297-308.

Wernz (1842-1914)-Vidal (1867-1938) [20] asserted that the Roman Ritual affects the whole Church, and consequently must now be followed. Wernz-Vidal wrote:

> "At attentis iteratis decretis S. R. C. et praxi eiusdem S. C. non amplius approbandi Ritualia dioecesana a Rituali Romano *distincta,* sed solummodo appendices vel *'Propria'* pro singulis dioecesibus, ex *disciplina vigente* potius tenendum est leges Ritualis Romani universalem afficere Ecclesiam." [21]

Other authors [22] believe that the Roman Ritual obliged all churches which were erected after its publication in 1614, and those churches which had been erected before its publication but which had left their own Ritual to follow the Roman Ritual.

Benedict XIV in 1752 and Pius X in 1913 reissued the Roman Ritual with several additions, but did not expressly prescribe its use as obligatory. However, Benedict XIV at least indirectly limited the power of bishops in publishing further Rituals, and greatly promoted the observance of the Roman Ritual, since in his list of prohibited books were included all editions that already were made or still were to be made of the Roman Ritual after its reformation by Paul V without the approval of the Sacred Congregation of Rites.[23]

The latest typical edition of the Roman Ritual was made in 1925 by order of Pope Pius XI, diligently revised, and accommodated to the norms of the new Code of Canon Law, to the Rubrics of the Roman Missal, and to the Decrees of the Apostolic See. It exists in a very handy form. It contains the decree by the Cardinal Prefect of the Sacred Congregation of Rites, in which the Pontifical approbation is comprised, but with no other preface than the Constitution *"Apostolicae Sedi"* of Paul V of June 17, 1614.[24]

At the present the rite of dedicating a church either by conse-

[20] *Ius Canonicum,* IV, pars 1, n. 338.

[21] Wernz-Vidal, *Ius Canonicum,* IV, pars 1, n. 338.

[22] Catalanus, *Rituale Benedicti* XIV, Prefatio; Van-Hove, *Prolegomena,* n. 242, footnote 2; Augustine, *Liturgical Law,* 10.

[23] Benedictus XIV, const. *"Quam ardenti,"* 25 mart. 1752—Found in the Preface of *Benedicti XIV Rituale Romanum.*

[24] S. R. C., 10 iun. 1925; *AAS,* XVII (1925), 326.

cration or by blessing is definitely set in the Roman Pontifical and the Roman Ritual. In view of canon 1257 [25] they must be used in the dedicatory ceremonies. The present Code legislation relative to the dedication of churches will be treated in the following chapters.

[25] Unius Apostolicae Sedis est tum sacram ordinare liturgiam, tum liturgicos approbare libros.

HISTORICAL SUMMARY

The early history of the canonical institute of the dedication of churches is shrouded in obscurity for lack of definite documents. However, this is no direct indication for denying that there was some sort of dedication of places used for divine worship before the peace of Constantine.

The theory which has been advanced that the dedication of churches is of Apostolic origin cannot be substantiated with authentic documents. If a dedicatory rite did exist prior to 313 it certainly could not be employed publicly because of the persecutions.

Numerous and definite documents attesting the dedication of churches can be found after the Edict of Tolerance given at Milan (313) by Constantine and Licinius.

The bishop of the territory was the ordinary minister of consecrating churches in his territory, and severe penalties were incurred by a bishop who consecrated a church outside of his territory without proper permission. The dedication of a church was so specially reserved to the office of a bishop that priests were not allowed to perform the consecration even under the pain of deposition from office, as is evident from the I Council of Braga (561). Pope Gregory IX (1227-1241) condemned the custom of some bishops who delegated simple priests to reconcile consecrated churches; *a fortiori,* a priest was not allowed to consecrate a church.

Every diocese had its particular usages, and thus the dedicatory rite was not at all uniform throughout the Church. Churches were dedicated with relics, or without relics if they were not obtainable, and even the celebration of Holy Mass seems to have been sufficient to dedicate a church. In 787 the VII Ecumenical Council, the II of Nicaea, was the first to pass general legislation requiring the consecration of churches which possessed relics.

At the end of the eleventh century one finds practically all the ceremonies described, as they are prescribed today in the Roman Pontifical for the dedication of churches. This was possible because of the diffusion of the Roman Sacramentaries and Ordinals, although the dedicatorial rite was not uniform, because whatever Sacramentary the bishop possessed, that also reflected the dedicatory rite which was used by the respective bishop in his diocese.

Pope Clement VIII in 1596 officially promulgated the *Pontificale Romanum* as the exclusive book for all Pontifical functions in the Western Church. All private Pontificals, whether approved or not, were suppressed and were to be replaced with the official *Pontificale Romanum.* An authoritative, uniform, and set rite to be used exclusively by all Latin bishops in the dedication of churches was had from that time.

It is impossible to point with certainty to the exact time when the Church introduced the distinction between the dedication of churches by consecration and the dedication of churches by blessing. At most it can be asserted that the distinction between the consecrating and blessing of churches definitely existed before the time of the promulgation of the Decretals of Gregory IX in 1234. Pope Sixtus V (1585-1590) on January 22, 1588, by his Constitution, *"Immensa"* [1] founded the *Congregatio pro sacris ritibus et caeremoniis,* consisting of five cardinals, with the task of: looking after the observance, improvement and correction of the liturgical books; settling disputes about precedence at processions and divine worship; and conducting the process of canonization and beatification. Questions and problems in regard to the dedication of churches were explained and settled by the Congregation established by Pope Sixtus V. Prior to the establishment of the Congregation by Pope Sixtus V, bishops used the Sacramentary they possessed, and the bishop in his diocese settled questions and problems in regard to the dedication of churches. The Congregation established by Pope Sixtus V was revised by Pope Pius X, and by his Constitution *Sapienti consilio,* on June 29, 1908, Pius X established the *Congregation of Sacred Rites.*[2] The competency of the Congregation of the Sacred Rites in regard to sacred rites and ceremonies of the Latin Church is reiterated in canon 253.

[1] *Bullarium Romanum,* VIII, 989-990.

[2] Pius X, const. *"Sapienti consilio,"* 29 iun. 1908—*Fontes,* n. 682.

PART TWO

THE CANONICAL COMMENTARY

INTRODUCTION

THE momentous merit of the present Code of Canon Law is the fact that pre-Code legislation and new legislation were crystallized and brought together in one place. Before the publication of the Code, legislation regarding the dedication of churches was scattered through the various decrees of the Sacred Congregation of Rites and in the Instructions of the Sacred Congregation for the Propagation of the Faith, and consequently was not readily or easily accessible to all.

Part II of the Third Book of the Code is entitled *"Of Sacred Places and Seasons,"* and is subdivided into two general sections. Section I deals with *Sacred Places,* and in turn is divided into 4 titles: (1) of churches; (2) of oratories; (3) of altars, and (4) of ecclesiastical burial. The last mentioned title is subdivided into 3 chapters: (1) of cemeteries; (2) of the transfer of the body to the church, of the funeral services, and of the interment; (3) of the persons to whom ecclesiastical burial is to be granted or denied. Section II, which deals with the sacred seasons, is divided into 2 titles: (1) of feast days, and (2) of abstinence and fasting.

The legislation of the Church in regard to sacred places is now found conveniently localized in Part II of the Third Book of the Code of Canon Law. Although there are other canons elsewhere in the Code which refer to sacred places, these canons are referred to in Part II of the Third Book.

It is to be acknowledged that the canons of the Code on sacred places and seasons are by no means completely new legislation. By far the most of the canons are pre-Code law condensed and written in clearer terms, at times even containing definitions, though the Code does not essay to furnish definitions for a goodly number of the terms it employs.

The rules of canon 6 must at all times be kept in mind if one wishes to interpret correctly the canons of the Code, for the norms expressed in canon 6 furnish the key to their proper interpretation and understanding. From canon 6 it is manifestly evident that the Code, even though it contains a number of new laws, was not intended to be a body of completely new laws, but that the old discipline was retained for the greater part with only slight modifications of the old law. Cicognani in commenting on canon 6 writes thus about the Code: [1]

> "It is the fountainhead of universal legislation, in such wise that the former discipline is no longer the immediate *source of legal authority*, but becomes a *source of interpretation*."

In commenting therefore on the Canons which deal with the consecration and blessing of churches, one must keep the above principles in mind. Quite frequently the canons in the Code must be interpreted in the light of the former legislation and according to the meaning which commentators attached to the law which existed prior to the Code. This must be done not only when the Code reproduces the former law unchanged, but whenever it is not certain that the present law has effected a change in the past legislation.[2]

[1] *Canon Law*, p. 499.

[2] Canon 6, 2°-4°.

CHAPTER VI

THE NECESSITY AND OBLIGATION OF CONSECRATING OR BLESSING A CHURCH

ARTICLE 1. ANCIENT DISCIPLINE

BEFORE the year 313, when the famous Edict of Tolerance was given at Milan by Constantine and Licinius, there is no definite document which refers to the necessity of dedicating churches, or other places used for worship. However, as was pointed out,[1] this is no direct indication for denying that there was some sort of dedication of places which were used for divine worship.

After the year 313 the dominant idea prevalent in the writings of the Fathers, in the general and particular councils, is that a church was not to be used as a place of worship, and especially the Holy Sacrifice was not to be offered in a new church, before the dedication of the church had taken place, unless great necessity compelled the use of the building. This is evident from the apology that St. Athanasius (+373) made for himself to the Emperor Constantius (+361) when he used an unfinished church at Alexandria for the Easter services before the church was dedicated.[2]

An Irish Council under St. Patrick (+c. 461) [3] as early as the middle of the fifth century advised priests who were building a church not to offer Mass in it before the bishop consecrated the church.

Pope Felix IV (526-530) [4] is quoted by Burchard, Bishop of Worms (1002-1005), in his *Decretum* (circa 1012),[5] and by Ivo, Bishop of Chartres (1090-1117), in his *Panormia* (circa 1095),[6] and

[1] Chapter II, Art. 1.

[2] Athanasius, *Apologia ad Imperatorem Constantium,* n. 14—*MPG,* XXV, 612.

[3] C. XXIII: "Si quis presbyterorum ecclesiam aedificaverit, non offerat, antequam adducat suum pontificem, ut eam consecret: quia sic decet."—Hardouin, I, 1792; Mansi, VI, 517.

[4] Jaffé, Regesta, n. 878.

[5] Lib. III, Cap. 57—*MPL,* CXL, 686.

[6] Lib. II, Cap. 33—*MPL,* CLXI, 1085.

in his *Decretum* (circa 1090-1095),[7] and these writers show that, because of the examples found in the Old Testament,[8] Christians dedicated their churches, as the Jews did their Temple, before using it for worship. Burchard and Ivo attach great importance to the necessity and obligation of dedicating the Christian churches, in which the Holiest and Sublimest of all Sacrifices is celebrated.

Gratian incorporated the same text in his *Decretum* (c. 1140),[9] showing the necessity of consecrating churches, and indicating that outside of the case of necessity Mass was not to be offered except in a church consecrated by a bishop. The passages incorporated by Gratian into his *Decretum*[10] are pseudo-Isidorian[11] nevertheless their value cannot be overlooked in as much as they reveal the norm of acting that must have been prevalent from the earliest period of Christianity in dedicating a church before using it for divine worship. Because of the persecutions, the dedicatory rite could not have been undertaken publicly from the establishment of the Church until the Edict of Milan (313). Authors[12] who do not admit the apostolic origin of dedicating churches, or are hesitant to do so because of the lack of authoritative documents prior to the Edict of Milan (313), do admit that some form of dedication for the places used for divine worship must have been employed even in the early days of the Church.[13]

In 787 the VII Ecumenical Council, the II General Council of Nicea was the first to pass general legislation to consecrate churches with relics. The Council further decreed that all churches which had been consecrated without the relics of martyrs should have relics

[7] Pars III, Cap. 60—*MPL,* CLXI, 204.

[8] Exodus XXXI; Numbers VII; Leviticus VIII; 2 Kings VII, XVI; 1 Paral. XXII; 3 Kings VIII.

[9] C. 1, 2, 11, D. I, *de cons.* Cf. also C. 3, 12, D. I, *de cons.*

[10] C. 1, 2, 11, D. I, *de cons.*

[11] Hinschius, *Decretales Pseudo-Isidorianae,* pp. 58, 698.

[12] Bingham, *The Antiquities of the Christian Church,* bk. VIII, chap. IX, sect. 1; Duchesne, *Christian Worship,* pp. 399-403; Many, *De Locis Sacris,* n. 10; Coronata, *De Locis et Temporibus Sacris,* n. 13; Catalanus, *Pontificale Romanum,* lib. II, tit. II, n. 1.

[13] See Chap. II, Art. 2, A, of this work (pp. 7-9).

placed in them with the customary prayers.[14] It is to be noted that the Council did not impose any obligation to consecrate churches, but simply enacted that churches were not to be consecrated without relics.

The Council of Mainz (888) [15] decreed that churches were to be consecrated. The Council of London (1237) [16] specified what churches were to be consecrated, and ordered that cathedral, conventual, and parochial churches were to be consecrated within two years from their completion, otherwise Mass could not be offered in those churches.

From two decretals of Pope Gregory IX (1227-1241) [17] it is evident that there were churches during his time that were not consecrated, but in which nevertheless divine worship was held. Likewise, even though a church had not been consecrated, it did not lose its privilege of immunity, for once Mass had been offered in the church, it was evidently considered dedicated to God.

The Council of Trent (1545-1563) did not directly legislate on the necessity or obligation of consecrating or blessing churches. The Council repeated ancient legislation that seculars and regulars were not to celebrate the sacrifice of Holy Mass in private homes, or entirely outside of a church or an oratory dedicated solely for divine worship.[18]

In the entire ancient discipline of the Church up to the time of the Council of Trent particular legislation can be found which demanded the dedication of churches, but no general legislation can be

[14] C. 7, Hardouin, IV, 491; Mansi, XIII, 751; Cf. Schroeder, *Disciplinary Decrees of the General Councils*, p. 148.

[15] C. 9—Mansi, XVIII, 67.

[16] C. 1—Mansi, XXIII, 447-448.

[17] "Si ecclesia *non consecrata* [italics not in the original] cuiuscunque semine fuerit aut sanguinis effusione polluta, aqua protinus exorcizata lavetur, ne divinae laudis in ea organa suspendantur: est tamen, quam citius fieri poterit consecranda."—C. 10, X, *de consecratione ecclesiae vel altaris*, III, 40: "Ecclesiae, in qua divina mysteria celebrantur, *licet adhuc non exstiterit consecrata* [italics not in the original], nullo iure privilegium immunitatis adimitur; quia obsequiis divinis dedicata nullius est temerariis ausibus profananda."—C. 9, X, *De immunitate ecclesiarum, coemiterii, et rerum ad eas pertinentium*, III, 49.

[18] Conc. Trident., Sess. XXII, *de observandis et evitandis in celebratione Missae;* Schroeder, *Canons and Decrees of the Council of Trent*, p. 150.

found which demanded the dedication of churches.[19] The Council of Trent decreed that Mass was to be offered only in a church or oratory which was dedicated solely for divine worship.

Article 2. Present Law

Canon 1165, § 1: Divina officia celebrari in nova ecclesia nequeunt, antequam eadem vel sollemni consecratione vel saltem benedictione divino cultui fuerit dedicata.

The present law is very clear about the necessity and obligation of dedicating new churches. The Code in the canon 1165, § 1, absolutely demands that new churches are to be dedicated for divine worship either through solemn consecration, or at least by means of a blessing; otherwise divine worship may not be held in the new church. This dedicatory rite may be performed in one of two ways: (1) by consecration; or (2) by blessing.

An observation to be made here is the following: To be specific in one's speech one should employ the words "consecration" or "blessing." To say merely that "a church was dedicated" simply means that it was set aside for divine worship. Without further explanation the statement lacks full information concerning whether the church was consecrated or blessed. Hence, the proper way of expressing the complete act of dedication consists in stating that the church was dedicated by consecration, or that it was dedicated by blessing. It is equally correct usage to speak of a church as being consecrated or blessed, for according to canon 1165, § 1, consecration and blessing are the only two ways by which a church can be dedicated for divine worship.

Canon 1165, § 1, uses the words *"divina officia."* The definition of these words is found in canon 2256, 1 °.[20] The divine offices imply those functions of the power of orders which by the institution of Christ or the Church are ordained for divine worship and can be

[19] Cf. Chapter II of this work, pp. 5-15.

[20] "Nomine divinorum officiorum intelliguntur functiones potestatis ordinis, quae de instituto Christi vel Ecclesiae ad divinum cultum ordinantur et a solis clericis fieri queunt."

performed by clerics only. Thus the Mass, the sacraments, preaching, and many other acts are comprised under the term *"divina officia."* [21]

Whatever acts therefore may be included in the term "divine offices," such acts may not be performed in a new church before it is consecrated or blessed. Thus permission from the local ordinary would be needed to preach in a new church that was not consecrated or blessed.

Canon 822, § 1: Missa celebranda est super altare consecratum et in ecclesia vel oratorio consecrato aut benedicto ad normam iuris, salvo praescripto can. 1196.

is a further argument for the necessity and obligation of consecrating or blessing a church or oratory before Mass is offered in it. The final qualifying clause in this canon points to canon 1196, which deals with the question of consecration or of blessing as relating to private and semi-public oratories.[22]

Under certain conditions stipulated by law the local ordinary, or when there is question of an exempt religious house the major superior, can give permission for a just and reasonable cause for the celebration of Mass outside of a church or oratory, but on a consecrated altar stone in a becoming place. This permission can be given only in an extraordinary case for one or the other time.[23]

Vermeersch (+1936)-Creusen [24] assert that an indult would be required to offer Mass in a church that has not been blessed. This

[21] Beste, *Introductio in Codicem,* pp. 915-916.

[22] The necessity and obligation of dedicating oratories is treated by Feldhaus, *Oratories,* The Catholic University of America Canon Law Studies, n. 42 (Washington, D. C.: The Catholic University of America Press, 1927), Chapters IX-X.

[23] Cf. canon 822, § 4; for an interpretation of the words *"per modum actus,"* cf. Bastnagel, "Cases and Studies"—*The Jurist,* II (1942), 155-158; Kinane, "The Meaning of 'Per Modum Actus' in Canon 822"—*The Irish Ecclesiastical Record,* XXV (1925), 425-426; Guiniven, *The Precept of Hearing Mass,* The Catholic University of America Canon Law Studies, n. 158 (Washington, D. C.: The Catholic University of America Press, 1942), pp. 126-132.

[24] *Epitome,* II, n. 482.

observation is true if a church were completed and no attempt were made to consecrate or bless it. Then indeed the bishop could not give permission to celebrate Mass in such a church, because, as Gasparri [25] correctly observes, the bishop may delegate a priest to bless the church if he is himself impeded from bestowing the blessing.

Many (+1922),[26] writing before the Code, held that Mass could be offered only for a time and with the express permission of the bishop in a church that was not blessed, namely, up to the time the blessing could take place, for in reality the church was already destined for divine worship and was considered as a sacred place.

It is generally admitted by authors [27] that divine worship may be permitted by a bishop in a "provisional church" which is not blessed, while the "definite church" is being built or repaired. Thus, in a practical case, if a church should burn or be destroyed by any other cause, or if a church should be in a state of repair, the local Ordinary may grant permission to hold divine services in a parish hall or any other decent place, while the "definitive church" is being built or repaired. The people of a parish or members of a community may not be deprived of divine services while their church is being built or repaired. Guiniven, in commenting on the words *"extraordinary cases"* and *"per modum actus"* of canon 822, § 4 writes:

> "The situations commonly existing in this country, such as the inability of a great number of the faithful to attend Mass on Sundays and Feastdays because of the limited capacity of the church, or because no church exists in the place, may be considered as 'extraordinary cases' justifying the grant of permission to celebrate Mass outside of a church or oratory.
>
> "*'Per modum actus'* must be strictly interpreted relative to the faculty of bishops to permit Mass outside of churches and oratories. In cases which will endure permanently or for a long period of time, the local Ordinary should apply to the Holy See for a special indult." [28]

[25] *De Ss. Eucharistia,* I, n. 155.

[26] *De Locis Sacris,* n. 19.

[27] Beste, *Introductio in Codicem,* p. 558; Coronata, *De Locis et Temporibus Sacris,* n. 21; Gasparri, *De Ss. Eucharistia,* I, n. 155; Vermeersch-Creusen, *Epitome,* II, n. 482.

[28] Guiniven, *The Precept of Hearing Mass,* p. 164.

In the case under consideration, namely when a *"definitive church"* is being built or repaired, the supposition is that the local Ordinary grants permission to hold divine services in a parish hall or any other decent place because he is assured that the "definitive church" will shortly be built or repaired, and the supposition is that the local Ordinary provides a "provisional church" only for the duration of the building or repairing of the "definitive church" in order that the people may not be deprived of divine services. Authors [29] admit that divine worship may be permitted by a bishop in a "provisional" church" which is not dedicated, while the "definitive church" is being built or repaired, but these authors are silent as to what should be done in regard to a case where the building of a "definitive church" will endure for a long period of time. Does canon 822, § 4 apply and may the Ordinary permit the celebration of Mass and other forms of divine worship in the "provisional building"? This writer follows Guiniven's explanation of the words *extraordinary cases* and *per modum actus* of canon 822, § 4, and holds that the Ordinary should apply to the Holy See for a special indult.[30] The factor of time will be relative and will differ in each case of the use of a "provisional church," hence the length of time during which the "provisional church" will be used will be the norm to guide the Ordinary in using the power of canon 822, § 4, or of having recourse to the Holy See.

A parish hall, an auditorium of a parish school, or any other decent place which is used as a "provisional church" for divine services cannot be blessed with the constitutive blessing of the Roman Ritual, *Ritus Benedicendi Novam Ecclesiam Seu Oratorium Publicum.* The canonical effect of dedication of a place by blessing is that the place becomes sacred and permanently deputed for acts of divine worship. This permanent deputation for divine services by the act of blessing is not realized in a "provisional church," since the "provisional church" will definitely be converted to secular use when the "defini-

[29] Beste, *Introductio in Codicem,* p. 558; Coronata, *De Locis et Temporibus Sacris,* n. 21; De Meester, *Juris Canonici et Juris Canonico-Civilis Compendium* (Nova editio, 3 vols. in 4, Brugis, 1921-1928), III, n. 1125, note 2.

[30] Guiniven, *The Precept of Hearing Mass,* pp. 121-132.

tive church" is built or repaired.[81] Before Mass is celebrated in the "provisional church" it should be blessed with the invocative blessing of *Benedictio Loci vel Domus*.[82] The *Benedictio Loci vel Domus* may be performed by any priest and at any time.[83]

If a new church were being built and because of some just and reasonable cause the consecration or blessing of the building were set for some not very distant date, it seems that in view of canon 822, § 4, and canon 1194, the bishop could permit the celebration of Mass in such a building on a consecrated altar stone, because the building is destined exclusively for divine worship.[84] If the bishop forsees that the blessing of a church will be put off for a notable length of time, then a priest should be delegated to bless the church, if the bishop is impeded from performing the act himself.[85]

Article 3. Classification of Churches to Be Consecrated or Blessed

Canon 1165, § 3: Solemni consecratione dedicentur ecclesiae cathedrales et, quantum fieri potest, ecclesiae collegiatae, conventuales, paroeciales.

This canon enacts for the first time a universal legislation which demands the dedication of cathedral churches by consecration. The same canon suggests also the dedication by consecration of collegiate, conventual, and parochial churches. The law in this canon does not mention dedication by blessing, because canon 1165, § 1, prohibits divine worship in a new church that has not been dedicated for divine worship at least by blessing.

Particular councils at times legislated on the necessity of consecrating certain churches. The Council of London in the year 1237

[81] Van Der Stappen, *Sacra Liturgia*, IV, pp. 455-466.

[82] *Rituale Romanum*, Tit. VIII, cap. 6.

[83] Van Der Stappen, *Sacra Liturgia*, IV, pp. 465-466; Collins, *The Church Edifice and Its Appointments* (2. ed., The Dolphin Press, Philadelphia, 1940), p. 26.

[84] Beste, *Introductio in Codicem*, p. 558; Coronata, *De Locis et Temporibus Sacris*, n. 21; Many, *De Locis Sacris*, n. 19.

[85] Canon 1165, § 1; Gasparri, *De Ss. Eucharistia*, n. 155.

in its first canon decreed that cathedral, conventual, and parochial churches were to be consecrated at least within two years from the time that they were completed.[36] Similarly the Council of Rome in the year 1725 [37] decreed that at least the cathedral and parochial churches erected in the dioceses belonging to the Province of Rome were to be consecrated within two years from the date of the celebration of that Council.

Canon 1165, § 3, specifically mentions cathedral, conventual, collegiate, and parish churches. A *cathedral church* is the church in which the bishop has permanently erected the episcopal throne. There are various species of cathedral churches, namely *primatial,* in which the throne of the primate is erected; *patriarchal,* in which the throne of the patriarch is erected; *metropolitan,* in which the throne of the metropolitan is erected; *episcopal,* in which the throne of the bishop is erected; *quasi-episcopal* or *quasi-cathedral,* in which the throne of a prelate or abbot *nullius* or of a vicar and prefect apostolic is erected.[38]

A *collegiate church* is one to which is attached a college or chapter of clerics or canons, and is called *insigne* or *perinsigne* if it has received that title by Apostolic privilege or by immemorial custom.[39] The Code in canon 391, § 1, explains the purpose of a chapter of clerics or of canons who form a body which is instituted for the purpose of the more solemn celebration of the divine service in their churches; the cathedral chapter has the additional purpose of assisting the bishop as his senate and council according to rules of Canon Law, and to administer the diocese during a vacancy.[40] A *conventual church,* also called a *regular* church, is one which is annexed to some

[36] Mansi, XXIII, 447-448.

[37] Tit. XXV, C. 1—*Acta et Decreta Sacrorum Conciliorum Recentiorum, Collectio Lacensis* (7 vols., Friburgi Brisgoviae, 1870-1892), I, 386. Hereafter cited as *Collectio Lacensis.*

[38] Beste, *Introductio in Codicem,* p. 556; Coronata, *De Locis et Temporibus Sacris,* n. 12; Many, *De Locis Sacris,* n. 62; Vermeersch-Creusen, *Epitome,* II, n. 476.

[39] Cf. canon 391, § 2. Beste, *Introductio in Codicem,* p. 556; Coronata, *De Locis et Temporibus Sacris,* n. 12; Many, *De Locis Sacris,* n. 62; Vermeersch-Creusen, *Epitome,* II, n. 476.

[40] Canon 391, § 1.

convent or monastery of a religious order or institute.[41] A *parochial church* is one which for the care of souls serves definite territorial limits, and has assigned to it by the bishop a pastor upon whom is incumbent the care of souls for the people of that territory.[42]

Pre-Code authors differed on the question of the necessity regarding which churches had to be consecrated. Suarez (+1617)[43] and Schmalzgrueber (+1735),[44] asserted that the properly so called consecration was not demanded for any church by the universal church law. Gatticus (+after 1752)[45] and Catalanus (+after 1757)[46] distinguished between major churches, namely cathedrals, and minor churches. They demanded consecration for the major churches only. Difficulties were present, however, for the above mentioned authors did not specifically determine what were major and what were minor churches. This controversy is settled now by the Code, inasmuch as canon 1165, § 3, demands the consecration of cathedral churches.

A. *Obligation to Consecrate Cathedral Churches*

The more solemn ceremonies of consecration are demanded by the Code for the dedication of a cathedral church, for it is the most important church in the diocese. In the cathedral church the bishop permanently erects the episcopal throne which is symbolical of the authority he exercises over the diocese.

Since canon 1165, § 3, demands the dedication of cathedral churches by means of a consecration, the various species of cathedral churches must be included under this general term, namely, the primatial, patriarchal, metropolitan, episcopal and quasi-episcopal churches.

[41] Beste, *Introductio in Codicem*, p. 556; Coronata, *De Locis et Temporibus Sacris*, n. 12; Many, *De Locis Sacris*, n. 62; Vermeersch-Creusen, *Epitome*, II, n. 476.

[42] Canon 216, §§ 1-3; Beste, *Introductio in Codicem*, p. 556; Coronata, *De Locis et Temporibus Sacris*, n. 12; Many, *De Locis Sacris*, n. 62; Vermeersch-Creusen, *Epitome*, II, n. 476.

[43] *De Eucharistia*, disp. LXXXI, sect. III.

[44] *Ius Ecclesiasticum Universum* (5 vols. in 12, Romae, 1843-1845), lib. III, tit. XL, n. 6.

[45] *De Oratoriis Domesticis* (Romae, 1770), 117.

[46] *Rituale Romanum*, tit. VIII, cap. XXIX, n. 8.

B. *Collegiate, Conventual, and Parish Churches Recommended to be Consecrated*

The Code does not strictly demand consecration for collegiate, conventual, and parochial churches, although a recommendation is given to consecrate them whenever possible.[47]

Before the Code, the Sacred Congregation of Rites [48] was asked with regard to a decree of the Council of Rome, held in the year 1725,[49] whether besides the cathedral and parochial churches, other public churches could be consecrated? To this query the Sacred Congregation replied that it was incumbent upon the bishops to consecrate at least the cathedral and parochial churches. Relative to the minor churches other than parochial churches, if the bishops did not desire to use their right of solemnly consecrating such churches, they were to give their faculty to priests to bless them.

Canon 1165, § 3, expresses the desire to have collegiate, conventual and parish churches consecrated. If that is impossible, then no matter what type of church it be, in order that divine worship be permitted in the new church building, the building must at least be dedicated by blessing, for which the bishop may delegate a priest. This same desire is expressed in the Roman Ritual:

> "Ecclesiae vero cathedrales, et, quantum fieri potest, ecclesiae collegiatae, conventuales, et paroeciales, quamvis a simplici Sacerdote, ut supra, sint benedictae, sollemniter tamen consecrandae sunt." [50]

The chief purpose of consecration or blessing is to withdraw the church from profane uses and to dedicate it to an exclusive religious use. Hence consecration and blessing have essentially the same

[47] Canon 1165, § 3: Sollemni consecratione dedicentur ecclesiae cathedrales et, *quantum fieri potest,* ecclesiae collegiatae, conventuales, paroeciales.

[48] 7 aug. 1875, ad 1—*Decr. Auth.,* n. 3364.

[49] Tit. XXV, C. 1—*Collectio Lacensis,* I, p. 386.
II, 2-3.

[50] Tit. VIII, Cap. 27, *Ritus Benedicendi Novam Ecclesiam seu Oratorium Publicum,* Rubric, n. 13.

canonical effect. The difference is in the solemnity, in the rite, and in the different requirements of law for consecration and for blessing. The difference between consecration and blessing will become more evident from a consideration of the various requirements of the law in relation to these distinct acts.

CHAPTER VII

CANONICAL REQUIREMENTS FOR THE CONSECRATION AND THE BLESSING OF CHURCHES

THE church occupies the most important place in the life of a Catholic, because in it the Holy Sacrifice of the Mass is celebrated; in the church the great Sacrament of the Body and Blood of Christ is preserved upon Catholic altars; and the church is used by all the faithful for all public religious services. Accordingly, Holy Mother Church has formulated regulations and placed certain requirements for the erection of churches. Before a church can be dedicated for divine worship in a permanent manner either by consecration or by blessing, certain conditions must be present and definite requirements of law must be observed. The requirements relative to consecration differ from the requirements for the blessing of a church. This distinction will become more evident from the considerations discussed in the following articles.

ARTICLE 1. CONSENT REQUIRED TO DEDICATE CHURCHES

Canon 1157: Non obstante quolibet privilegio, nemo potest locum sacrum consecrare vel benedicere sine Ordinarii consensu.

No one can consecrate or bless places without the consent of the proper ecclesiastical authority to whom the consecration or blessing is reserved. Canon 1157 uses the term *"ordinary,"* and not *"local ordinary,"* for in exempt clerical institutes no one can *bless* a place belonging to them without the consent of the major superior of the exempt clerical institute. The Code does not recognize any privilege against this right of the respective ordinary.[1]

Authors [2] are in agreement that the dedication by consecration

[1] " . . . *non obstante quolibet privilegio.*"

[2] Augustine, *A Commentary on Canon Law,* VI, 7; Aloisius, Barin, "Commentarium ad Canones C. I. C. sacram Liturgiam spectantes"—*Ephemerides*

of a church, even of one which belongs to an exempt clerical institute, pertains to the local ordinary; and even regulars whose superior enjoys episcopal consecration must have recourse to the local ordinary for the consecration of their own proper churches. The right of the exempt clerical religious superior to *bless* his church is protected by canon 1157, but at the same time the authority of the local ordinary for the consecration of churches is safeguarded by the rule of canon 1155, § 1:

> **Consecratio alicuius loci, quanquam ad regulares pertinentis, spectat ad Ordinarium territorii in quo locus ipse reperitur, dummodo Ordinarius charactere episcopali sit insignitus, non tamen ad Vicarium Generalem sine speciali mandato, firmo iure S.R.E. Cardinalium consecrandi ecclesiam et altaria sui tituli.**

Ayrinhac (+1930) [3] implies that a bishop does not need the consent of the exempt clerical religious superior to dedicate by consecration a church which is located in his territory, but which belongs to an exempt order; however, he fails to adduce any reasons or arguments.[4]

Jone,[5] in commenting on canon 1155, § 1, states that regulars are mentioned because they themselves, along with their churches and houses, are exempt according to canon 615. But, as is evident from canon 1157 which states that in order to consecrate or bless a place the permission of the competent ordinary is necessary, the bishop may not consecrate a place of the regulars, if the ordinary of the

Liturgicae (Roma, Via Pompeo Magno, 21), XXXVI (1922), 16-17 (hereafter this article will be cited as Barin, "Commentarium"); Beste, *Introductio in Codicem*, p. 554; Coronata, *De Locis et Temporibus Sacris*, n. 5; Wernz-Vidal, *Ius Canonicum*, IV, *De Rebus*, pars I, 441; Woywod, *A Practical Commentary*,

[3] *Administrative Legislation*, n. 4.

[4] "Some think that a bishop would need the permission of the superior lawfully to consecrate a church located in his territory but belonging to an exempt order (Vermeersch, n. 47). This does not, however, seem to be the meaning of this canon (1157)."—Ayrinhac, *loc. cit.*

[5] *Gesetzbuch des kanonischen Rechtes* (3 vols., Paderborn: Ferdinand Schöningh, 1939-1941), II, 358.

regulars does not give his consent.[6] Hence, the local ordinary may not consecrate the church of an exempt clerical order if the ordinary of that order does not give his consent, for, according to canon 615, the local ordinary has no jurisdiction over the church that belongs to the exempt order. On the other hand, according to canon 1155, the religious ordinary must have the local ordinary consecrate a church that belongs to the order, or, if the religious ordinary has the episcopal character and desires to perform the consecration himself, he must get the permission of the local ordinary.[7]

To dedicate a church by blessing, the religious ordinary is not in need of the permission or consent of the local ordinary, when the church that is to be blessed belongs to the exempt order.[8]

Canon 1157 states that *non obstante quolibet privilegio* no one may consecrate or bless a sacred place without the consent of the ordinary. Under the former law, if the local ordinary was petitioned with due reverence to consecrate a church (or an altar) for regulars, and then refused to perform the consecration after repeated requests made with due reverence and courtesy, the regulars were permitted to call in another bishop according to a privilege granted by Pope Leo X at the V General Lateran Council (1512-1517).[9] From this privilege it followed that, if the local ordinary was petitioned "twice or three times" to consecrate a church of exempt regulars, and then refused, the religious superior could consecrate the church himself if endowed with the episcopal character, or, lacking the episcopal character, he could invite another bishop to perform the consecration.

Canon 1155, § 1, decrees that the local ordinary has the right to consecrate places in his territory, even those that belong to exempt religious organizations. This explains why regulars, even if their superior enjoys episcopal powers, must have recourse to the local ordinary for the consecration of their churches. Beste[10] further

[6] Canon 198, §§ 1-2, makes it unmistakable that a major superior in a clerical exempt religious institute is to be classed as an ordinary.

[7] Cf. canon 1155, § 1.

[8] Cf. canons 1156 and 1157.

[9] Const. *"Dum intra,"* 19 dec. 1516, § 12—*Fontes,* I, n. 72.

[10] *Introductio in Codicem,* p. 553.

clarifies the position of the local ordinary. A religious ordinary, even when he is a bishop, must appeal to the local ordinary in view of the latter's exclusive right before he consecrates his own proper church. Pre-Code and Code authors agree that the consecration of a church, even of one which belongs to an exempt religious organization, pertains to the local ordinary. The authors are divided on the continued existence of the privilege granted to regulars by Pope Leo X in the Constitutio *Dum intra* of December 19, 1516, in virtue of which the superior of exempt clerical regulars, who had petitioned the local ordinary two or three times to consecrate their church and had then been refused by him, could consecrate the church himself if he was endowed with the episcopal character, or, lacking the episcopal character, could invite another bishop to perform the consecration without any consent of the local ordinary. Pre-Code authors like Gasparri (+1934) [11] and Many (+1922) [12] maintained that the privilege granted to regulars by Leo X was not revoked by the Council of Trent (sess. VI, *de ref.*, c. 5; sess. XIV, *de ref.*, c. 2). Code authors are divided: Augustine [13] and Coronata [14] maintain that the privilege is not revoked by canon 1157; Coronata [15] follows Many [16] a pre-Codè author in claiming that the privilege is still in force.

> "Igitur suam vim retinet privilegium quo plures Regulares poterant loca consecrare per quemlibet Episcopum, si petitam prius consecrationem ab Ordinario loci, iste ultra sex menses distulisset." [17]

Ayrinhac,[18] Blat,[19] Vermeersch-Creusen,[20] and Woywod [21] maintain

[11] *De Ss. Eucharistia,* I, n. 157.

[12] *De Locis Sacris,* n. 12.

[13] *A Commentary on Canon Law,* VI, 7.

[14] *De Locis et Temporibus Sacris,* n. 5.

[15] *De Locis et Temporibus Sacris,* n. 5.

[16] *De Locis Sacris,* n. 12.

[17] Coronata, *De Locis et Temporibus Sacris,* n. 5.

[18] *Administrative Legislation,* nn. 2 and 4.

[19] *Commentarium,* III, n. 3.

[20] *Epitome,* II, n. 471.

[21] *A Practical Commentary,* II, 2-3.

that in virtue of canon 1157 the privilege is revoked. To avoid dissensions and misunderstandings if difficulties should arise between the local ordinary and regulars over the consecration of churches recourse should be made to the Holy See.

A. *When Is Consent to Consecrate or to Bless a Church to Be Denied?*

The dedication of a church either by consecration or by blessing is a sacred rite instituted by the Church, in virtue of which a profane place is rendered sacred, and is permanently destined by a lawful minister for the use of the faithful for the purpose of divine worship.[22]

The Code in canon 1165, § 2, rules:

> **Si prudenter praevideatur ecclesiam conversum iri ad usus profanos, Ordinarius consensum eius aedificationi ne praebeat, aut saltem, si forte aedificata fuerit, eam ne consecret neve benedicat.**

If the ordinary prudently forsees that the church will be turned to profane uses *(ad usus profanos)*, he shall not give his consent to have the church built, or, if it is erected, he shall not consecrate or bless the church. Such a prudent fear would exit, if the church belonged to a private family and thus could pass into the hands of persons less favorably disposed toward the Church, or if, because of the debt and mortgage on which payment is uncertain, the church would be liable to a transfer of ownership and the ultimate employment of it for secular uses by way of sale or alienation.

The Sacred Congregation of Rites [23] was asked if it were lawful to consecrate a church that belonged to a private family, and which according to existing civil laws could be transferred or sold in a hereditary manner by a will, or turned to secular use. The Sacred Congregation of Rites replied that unless sufficient guarantees were

[22] Beste, *Introductio in Codicem*, p. 558; Coronata, *De Locis et Temporibus Sacris*, n. 21; Vermeersch-Creusen, *Epitome*, II, n. 482; Wernz, *Ius Decretalium*, III, n. 436.

[23] *In Taurinen.*, 4 maii 1882, ad II—*Decr. Auth.*, n. 3546.

had against the mentioned eventualities, such a church should not be consecrated.[24]

B. *Meaning of "Ad Usum mere Profanum."*

Consent to build a church, or to consecrate or bless a church is to be denied if the ordinary prudently forsees that the church building will be used for merely secular uses. What is to be understood by the words *"ad usum mere profanum"?* A consideration of various decisions given by the Sacred Congregation of Rites will help to determine the meaning of these words.

The Sacred Congregation of Rites [25] did not approve of a dormitory above a church to be used by clerics or religious. The same Sacred Congregation [26] did not approve of a wine cellar, or the keeping of oil and other provisions *(res mere profanas)* under the church. The Sacred Congregation [27] decreed that the basement or the hall of a church may not be used for merely secular meetings or entertainments, even if the basement were used only as a theatre for school children.

Unquestionably the words *"ad usum mere profanum"* connote all such activities as dances, balls, banquets, bingo parties, card parties or bazaars held in the church basement.[28] Natural and ecclesiastical law forbid affairs which, although lawful in themselves, are not in keeping with the holiness of places of worship. Secular theatrical productions, banquets, noisy gatherings, mundane discussions, secular trials either civil or criminal, were excluded from taking place in a place of worship.[29] Custom in some countries allowed theological disputations, literary exercises, musical concerts,

[24] *"In casu, de quo agitur, nisi habeantur sufficientes cautiones, abstinendum ab huiusmodi ecclesiae consecratione."—Decr. Auth., loc. cit.*

[25] 11 maii 1641—*Decr. Auth.*, n. 756.

[26] S. R. C., 31 aug. 1867, ad V—*Decr. Auth.*, n. 3157.

[27] S. R. C., 4 maii 1882, ad I—*Decr. Auth.*, n. 3546.

[28] Augustine, *A Commentary on Canon Law*, VI, 18-19; Ayrinhac, *Administrative Legislation*, n. 23; Beste, *Introductio in Codicem*, p. 558; Many, *De Locis Sacris*, n. 44; Wernz, *Ius Decretalium*, III, n. 447.

[29] C. 2, *de immunitate ecclesiarum, coemeteriorum et aliorum locorum religiosorum*, III, 23, in VI°.

school commencements or academic meetings to be held in churches.[30] What may appear to be unbecoming in one locality is not necessarily viewed as such in another, and hence by legislation and custom certain practices may be tolerated. It is beyond the scope of this dissertation to judge if certain practices are in direct opposition to the Code.[31]

Authors [32] do not include under the phrase *"ad usum mere profanum"* the fact that the space above or below a church is used to store things which pertain to divine worship, or that the space is used as a parish library, or as a library for a religious house. Likewise the use of such a space for sodality meetings, for religious conferences, or for a parish school, provided that the scope is religious in purpose, cannot be designated as a secular use. The end or aim for which the space below or above the church is to be used will be a telling factor for the local ordinary in judging whether or not the church building is being or will be employed *"ad usum mere profanum,"* and whether according to canon 1165, § 2, he is to withhold his consent for the consecration or blessing of the church.

C. *Consecration and Blessing of Combination Buildings*

In many parts of this country one finds the so-called combination buildings (church and school combined in one building). The church may occupy the top portion of the building, and the parochial school the lower portion of the building, or vice versa. If one prescinds from the question whether such combination buildings are erected in full accord with the legislation of the Code, it is of interest, since such buildings exist in various dioceses of this country, to know whether the church in a combination building may be dedicated by consecration or blessing.

Canon 1164, § 2, states that the space below the floor or above

[30] Wernz, *Ius Decretalium,* III, n. 447.

[31] On the above matter the reader is referred to: E. J. M., "Parish Hall in Church Basement"—*The Clergy Review,* XXII (1942), 131-132.

[32] Ayrinhac, *Administrative Legislation,* n. 11; Beste, *Introductio in Codicem,* p. 558; Jone, *Gesetzbuch des kanonischen Rechtes,* II, 362; Woywod, *A Practical Commentary,* II, 7.

the ceiling of the church, if there be any, shall not be used for purely secular uses.[33]

Canon 1165, § 2, states that, if it can be reasonably foreseen that a church will be turned to a secular use, the ordinary shall not give his consent for the building of the church, or, if it has already been built, he shall not consecrate or bless the church.

Authors[34] state that the parish school which is housed in the space below or above a church certainly does not come under the scope of the phrase *"ad usum mere profanum."* In a combination building a set and definite portion of the building is destined as the church, and likewise a set and definite portion of the building is destined as the parochial school. If all other requirements of law are observed, there seems to be no objection to the dedication of the church in such a combination building, either by consecration or by blessing. If, however, in the combination building, just as well as in a church building, part of the building were used as the living quarters of sisters, or as an auditorium for plays, entertainments, etc., the church in such a combination building could not, according to canon 1164, § 2, and canon 1165, § 2, be consecrated or blessed. The church building cannot be used for the secular purposes described above and hence any such secular uses of the church building must first be abolished before the church can be dedicated. The writer believes that the deciding factor in determining whether a church in a combination building may be consecrated or blessed derives from the purpose of the building itself. If the combination building is used merely to house the church and the parochial school, there does not seem to be any legal prohibition against consecrating or blessing the church of such a combination building, provided that the other requirements of law for consecration or blessing are observed. A legal prohibition against consecrating or blessing the church in a combination building could be adduced only when there would be a

[33] "*. . . locaque, si adsint, subter ecclesiae pavimentum aut supra ecclesiam, ad usum mere profanum ne adhibeantur.*"

[34] Ayrinhac, *Administrative Legislation,* n. 11; Beste, *Introductio in Codicem,* p. 558; Jone, *Gesetzbuch des kanonischen Rechtes,* II, 362; Woywod, *A Practical Commentary,* II, 7; Augustine, *A Commentary on Canon Law,* VI, 18.

use of the building *"ad usum mere profanum,"* as explained in Art. 1, B, of this chapter.

Augustine [35] writes: "There is a difference between consecration and blessing and we hardly believe that a combination building could be consecrated." The writer agrees with Augustine that there is a difference between consecration and blessing, but disagrees with him that a combination building can not be *consecrated.* If the combination building is used merely as a church and school—and Augustine himself admits that the phrase *"ad usum mere profanum"* cannot be made to refer to a parish school above or below a church [36]—the writer fails to see why the church in a combination building may not be *consecrated.* For argument's sake, one may raise the question whether a church in a combination building can be blessed. Blessing is one way of dedicating a church, and consecration is but another way. The legal effects of consecrating or of blessing a church are the same, namely, the building becomes a sacred place, and a fit place for divine worship.[37] The difference between the dedication of a church by consecration and the dedication of a church by blessing is in the greater or lesser solemnity of rite attached by the Church to the act of dedication. Hence, if a church in a combination building may be dedicated by blessing, that same church may also be dedicated by consecration if the other legal requirements are observed. This is even suggested by the Roman Ritual [38] which prescribes: *"Ecclesiae . . . quamvis a simplici Sacerdote, ut supra, sint benedictae, sollemniter tamen consecrandae sunt."*

D. *Consecration of Churches in Debt*

A question of importance is the following: Must a church be free of all debt before the bishop can dedicate the church by consecration?

Canon 1165, § 2, rules that if the ordinary prudently foresees that the church will be turned over to secular use, he shall not give his consent: (1) to build the church, or (2) to consecrate or bless the

[35] *A Commentary on Canon Law,* VI, 18.

[36] Augustine, *A Commentary on Canon Law,* VI, 18.

[37] Cf. canons 1154 and 1165, § 1.

[38] *Rituale Romanum,* Tit. VIII, Cap. 27, n. 13.

church if the church is already erected. The reason for this ruling of the Code is evident. The church building is intended as a sacred place, to be set aside for divine worship exclusively and permanently by acts of either consecration or blessing. If there is any danger that the church building will be used for any other purpose than that of divine worship, the local ordinary must deny his consent to have the church built, or, if it is erected, he may not consecrate or bless the church.

The Sacred Congregation of Rites [89] was asked if it were lawful to *consecrate* a church that belonged to a private family, and which, according to existing civil laws of the place, could be transferred in a hereditary manner by will, or turned over to secular use by sale. The Sacred Congregation of Rites replied: "In casu, de quo agitur, nisi habeantur sufficientes cautiones, abstinendum ab huiusmodi Ecclesiae consecratione." This response was given in a particular case, and hence it does not directly have the force of a universal application. The response is important, however, insofar as it shows the intention of the Holy See that churches which are in danger of being turned over to a secular use are not to be consecrated.

The writer was unable to find any direct prohibition in the Code, or in the general legislation of the Church previous to the Code, or in any decrees of the Sacred Congregation of Rites, to the effect that a church had to be free of debt before the bishop could consecrate it. Canon 1165, § 2, and the response of the Sacred Congregation of Rites quoted above prohibit the consecration of a church if there is danger that the building will be put to secular uses. As long as this danger is absent, even if there be a debt on the church, the writer believes that the bishop may consecrate such a church.

In certain countries or localities plenary and provincial councils, or diocesan synodal decrees may forbid the consecration of a church which is in debt. That would be a particular law, since there is no such prohibition in the Code. The reason for such a particular law is given by Nevin when he writes: "In a country where the Catholic Faith is the object of persecution or hostility, a heavy mortgage or debt on a church might involve the risk of being seized and converted

[89] S. R. C., 4 maii 1882, ad II—*Decr. Auth.*, n. 3546.

to profane uses." [40] Fortescue-O'Connell write: "In England and Ireland many churches are not consecrated, but simply blessed. . . . A church may be blessed at first, then consecrated later, when it is free of debt." [41] England and Ireland may have particular laws forbidding the consecration of churches which are in debt, but the assertion of Fortescue-O'Connell that "consecration is not allowed until the (church) building is free of debt and mortgage," has no legal foundation in the general law of the Church. At most such a requirement may be consequent to a particular law for England and Ireland. It is impossible to trace the origin of the widespread belief among the clergy that a church cannot be consecrated unless it is free of debt, apart from particular laws to the effect the belief lacks legal foundation.[42]

In America the churches are erected and sustained by the free-will contributions of the faithful, and in compliance with the Code [43] bishops do not give their consent for the erecting of a church unless they prudently foresee that actual capital assets as held by the moral personality responsible for the payment are had to build a church, and that later there will also be the necessary means for maintaining the church building, for supporting the ministers and for defraying the other expenditures of religious worship. Usually a sum of money proportionate to the total cost of the church building is a necessary prerequisite before the bishop will give his consent for the erection of the church. If there is some debt remaining on the church—and usually there is—, but the bishop is assured that the debt is being lowered yearly by the free contributions of the faithful, by pledges made by the faithful, or by other means, this seems to afford the *"sufficientes cautiones"* which will entitle the bishop to consecrate such a church even though there may be a debt on the church building. Each case merits the special attention and scrutiny of the

[40] "Heavy Debt on Church—May Altar Be Consecrated"—*The Australasian Catholic Record,* XV (1938), 259-260. Hereafter cited *ACR.*

[41] *The Ceremonies of the Roman Rite Described* (6. ed., London: Burns, Oates & Washbourne, Ltd., 1937), p. 1.

[42] Cf. Nevin, "Heavy Debt on Church—May Altar Be Consecrated"—*ACR,* XV (1938), 260.

[43] Canons 1162, § 2, and 1165, § 2.

local ordinary before consent is given for the consecration of a church which is in debt. The same rule applies to the blessing of a church.

Consecration is one form of dedicating a church for divine worship, but a church may also be dedicated for divine worship by blessing.[44] The Code does not mention the fact that a church must be free of debt to be either consecrated or blessed. If a church in debt could not be consecrated, it likewise would follow that a church in debt could not be blessed, for consecration and blessing have the same canonical effect, namely, the setting aside of a place for an exclusive religious use as a sacred place.[45]

In confirmation of the statement that a church which is in debt may be consecrated, a very practical observation is offered by Nevin. He states that "the blessing or consecration of a church would not of itself exclude the possibility of mortgage, provided the sacred use and purpose of the church be safeguarded." [46]

Stenger points out that church property is mortgageable even though it is blessed or consecrated, and further insists that the idea of requiring a *consecrated* church to be debt-free is unfounded in the general law.[47] A logical deduction is offered by Stenger:[48] if a consecrated church must remain debt-free and cannot be mortgaged, then a blessed church would also have to remain debt-free and could not be mortgaged. He writes:

> "Both these conclusions are unjustified. The only licit parallel would be this: that if the debt to be imposed on a consecrated or blessed church is so great that it is prudently foreseen the

[44] Canon 1165, § 1: Divina officia celebrari in nova ecclesia nequeunt, antequam eadem vel sollemni consecratione vel saltem *benedictione* divino cultui fuerit dedicata.

[45] Cf. canon 1154.

[46] Nevin, "A Mortgage on the Parochial Church"—*ACR*, X (1933), 348-351.

[47] *The Mortgaging of Church Property,* The Catholic University of America Canon Law Studies, No. 169 (Washington, D. C.: The Catholic University of America Press, 1942), p. 20.

[48] *Op. cit.*, p. 21; cf. also Heston, *The Alienation of Church Property in the United States,* The Catholic University of America Canon Law Studies, No. 132 (Washington, D. C.: The Catholic University of America Press, 1941), pp. 69-91 and pp. 160-174.

church will be turned over to profane usage as a result of the debt, the debt could not be contracted. This would be against all sound business principles besides, since a mortgage should ordinarily not be greater than sixty per cent of the actual value of the building. Moreover, in permitting the mortgage to be contracted, the ordinary before giving permission must know how and within what time the debt will be removed. Naturally, if there is no possible means of removing the debt it should not be contracted."[49]

Article 2. Material Construction of Churches to be Consecrated or Blessed

Consecration and blessing of a sacred place have the same legal effect, namely, to withdraw the place from profane use and dedicate it permanently for an exclusive religious use.[50] Consecration and blessing differ chiefly in their solemnity and rite. That the Church attaches more importance to the dedication of a church by consecration is evident from canon 1165, § 4, which rules that a church built of wood, iron, or any other metal may be blessed, but cannot be consecrated.

Canon 1165, § 4: Ecclesia ex lingo vel ferro aliove metallo benedici potest, non autem consecrari.

The factor of the permanency of a building is no doubt one of the reasons for the Code's ruling. In order that a church be consecrated it must be built of stone, brick, or reinforced concrete. Formerly there was some doubt if a church built of *"coemento armato"* (reinforced concrete) could be consecrated. However, the Sacred Congregation of Rites[51] decreed that a church built of reinforced concrete could be consecrated provided that the places for the twelve anointed crosses on the walls and the door posts at the main entrance of the church are of stone.

If a church built of wood were merely reinforced and covered with asbestos-cement siding, which is made in different shapes, similar to the usual wood siding, or in a wood shingle shape, or also

[49] Stenger, *The Mortgaging of Church Property*, p. 21.
[50] Cf. canons 1154 and 1165, § 1.
[51] 12 nov. 1909—*Decr. Auth.*, n. 4240.

in the brick-type, such a building could only be blessed but not consecrated, since the building itself must still be considered built of wood, even though it is covered with the above described asbestos-cement siding, or any other material similar to it. A church built with a surface of stucco could be blessed, but not consecrated, since stucco is not a durable material and cracks very easily and even if the stucco were very durable, the church would still not be a church built of stone, brick, or concrete. A wooden church overlaid by any shingling material for the purpose both of prolonging the life of the wooden building and also of doing away with the necessity of future paint jobs could only be blessed, but not consecrated.

In our modern day when many new building materials are being produced to add to the life of a building, or even to be used as actual building material, the law nevertheless insists that only churches which are built of stone, brick, or reinforced concrete may be consecrated. In different sections of the country, new building materials suited to the climatic conditions of the locality have been developed, and are found very satisfactory in church building. In a case of doubt about the possible consecration of a church built from material besides stone, brick, or reinforced concrete, the Holy See should be petitioned to solve the doubt. Perhaps there are used in certain sections of the world other building materials besides stone, brick, or reinforced concrete which, if the matter were explained to the Holy See, would not bar the consecration of the church.

The use of glass in our everyday life is opening an era and realm of great possibilities. Extensive experiments conducted with glass may open up for the future the possibility of glass buildings. If this should become a reality, the Holy See will have to be petitioned to find out if such a building may be dedicated, and if the dedication is to be by blessing, or by consecration.

Article 3. Time of Consecration or Blessing of Churches

The consecration of churches may take place on any day.

Canon 1166, § 1: Ecclesiarum consecratio, quamvis quolibet die fieri possit, decentius tamen dominicis aliisve festis de praecepto peragitur.

This is a repetition of the Decretal law.[52] Sundays and holydays of obligation are, however, more properly suited days.[53]

Although it is allowed on any day to consecrate a church, Sundays or Feastdays of obligation should be chosen as being more suitable for this solemn function, and enabling a greater number of the faithful to attend the ceremonies.[54] Holydays of obligation must be understood as mentioned and described in canon 1247.

Canon 1166, § 1 mentions the time simply for the consecration of churches, but is silent in regard to the time for the blessing of churches. The rubrics of the Roman Ritual are also silent as to when the blessing of a church may take place. One thing is certain from the rubrics of the Roman Ritual, namely, that Holy Mass must be offered after the church is blessed.[55] Hence, the ceremony of blessing a church must take place at such a time when it will be possible to offer Mass after the dedicatory services are completed.[56]

There is a greater liberty allowed in regard to the time for the blessing of a church than for its consecration. Although the consecration of a church may take place on any day, the Code [57] desires the consecration of a church to take place on a Sunday or any other Feastday of obligation, as being a day which is more becoming for the solemn ceremony of consecration. That is the legislator's desire or wish. But the blessing of a church can also be performed on any day besides Sunday or a Feastday of obligation, according to the legal maxim, "quod legislator voluit expressit." The preference expressed in the case of the consecration of a church is not indicated as extending to the blessing.

[52] "In dioecesi tua licet tibi ecclesiis dedicationem impendere tam diebus dominicis quam privatis."—C. 2, X, *de consecratione ecclesiae vel altaris,* III, 40.

[53] Canon 1166, § 1: . . . decentius tamen diebus dominicis aliisve festis de praecepto peragitur. Cf. *Pontificale Romanum,* tit., *De ecclesiae dedicatione seu consecratione.*

[54] Barin, "Commentarium"—*Ephemerides Liturgicae,* XXXVII (1923), 58.

[55] Rituale Romanum, Tit. VIII, Cap. 27, *Ritus benedicendi novam ecclesiam seu oratorium publicum,* n. 12.

[56] Cf. canons 820 and 821, § 1.

[57] Canon 1166, § 1.

Article 4. Fast Preceding the Consecration of Churches

Canon 1166, § 2, states:

> **Episcopus consecrans et qui petunt ecclesiam sibi consecrari, per eum diem qui consecrationem praecedit, ieiunent.**

The Roman Pontifical decrees:

> **Quando autem Ecclesia fuerit dedicanda, debet Archidiaconus praenuntiare clero et populo, quibus est Ecclesia consecranda; ut priusquam consecretur, ieiunent. Nam Pontifex consecrans, et qui petunt sibi Ecclesiam consecrari, praecedenti die ieiunare debent.**[58]

The consecrating bishop and those who ask for the consecration of a church must fast on the day previous to the consecration. The Sacred Congregation of Rites decreed that the fast on the day preceding the consecration of a church is of strict obligation for the consecrating bishop and for those who ask that the church be consecrated.[59]

If a pastor requests that the parochial church be consecrated, he certainly is bound to fast. Are the parishioners bound to fast? Inherently they are not bound to fast, since usually it is the pastor alone who requests the consecration of the church.[60] But if the matter were decided by a vote of the parishioners to have the church consecrated, or if the parishioners influenced the pastor to request the bishop to consecrate the church, then indeed the pastor and all the parishioners including those who might have opposed the consecration are bound by the fast.[61]

[58] Pontificale Romanum, Tit., *De ecclesiae dedicatione seu consecratione.*

[59] S. R. C., 29 iul. 1780, ad I—*Decr. Auth.*, n. 2519.

[60] Beste, *Introductio in Codicem,* p. 559; Vermeersch-Creusen, *Epitome,* II, n. 483.

[61] S. C. C., *Buscoducen,* 3 iul. 1909—*Fontes,* VI, n. 4354. Cf. S. R. C., *Mechlinien,* 29 iul. 1870—*Fontes,* n. 5818; Beste, *Introductio in Codicem,* p. 559; Coronata, *De Locis et Temporibus Sacris,* n. 23.

Similarly, if the superior of a religious community alone requests the consecration of a church, then he alone is held by the fast. But if the community makes the request as a body, then all, including those who might have voted against the consecration, are bound by the fast.[62]

Coronata,[63] following Gasparri,[64] holds that the obligation of fast applies to all the clergy belonging to the church. Hence a parochial adjutant or a parochial assistant would be bound by the fast. But this does not seem to be in accord with the meaning of canon 1166, § 2, which states: "*Episcopus consecrans et qui petunt ecclesiam sibi consecrari, . . . ieiunent.*" Ordinarily the assistants have no voice in the matter of requesting the consecration of a church, but the whole action rests with the pastor, and he alone requests the consecration. Therefore, he alone is obliged to observe the fast, and not the assisting clergy.[65]

The Sacred Congregation of Rites in two responses[66] declared: "Ieiunium a Pontificali Romano praescriptum esse strictae obligationis pro episcopo consecrante et '*pro iis tantum*' qui petunt ecclesiam sibi consecrari." Since the assistant does not ask for the consecration of a church to which he is attached, he cannot be included in the words "*qui petunt ecclesiam sibi consecrari . . . ieiunent.*"[67] Hence he is not obliged to observe the fast.[68]

62 Beste, *Introductio in Codicem*, p. 559; Vermeersch-Creusen, *Epitome*, II, n. 483.

63 *De Locis et Temporibus Sacris*, n. 23.

64 *De Ss. Eucharistia*, I, n. 163.

65 "Ad hoc ieiunium servandum non alii tenentur amplius praeter Episcopum consecrantem et eos qui petunt ecclesiam sibi consecrari, iuxta can. 1166, § 2; cessavit ideo obligatio quae olim adstringebat quoque clerum et populum. Nec ad ieiunandum tenentur qui nondum expleverint vicesimum primum aetatis annum (canon 1254, § 2)"—Maroto, "De ieiunio in consecratione ecclesiae"—*Apollinaris*, III (1930), 238.

66 29 iul. 1780—*Decr. Auth.*, n. 2519; 12 sept. 1840—*Decr. Auth.*, n. 2821.

67 Canon 1166, § 2; Cf. S. C. C., *Buscoducen.*, 3 iul. 1909—*AAS*, I (1909), 623-625; *Fontes*, n. 4354.

68 Ayrinhac (*Administrative Legislation*, n. 14) states that the clergy and people are not bound by the fast, if they had nothing to do with the request for the consecration of the church.

A chaplain of a religious community of sisters is not bound by the fast if in the name of the sisters he requests the bishop to consecrate their church.[69] If the chaplain of his own accord after talking the matter over with the sister superior asked for the consecration, the chaplain would also be bound to observe the fast.[70]

The *Pontifical Commission* for the Interpretation of the Code was asked if the fast preceding the consecration of a church, which is mentioned in canon 1166, § 2, is to be regulated according to the common law of the ecclesiastical fast? The reply was in the affirmative.[71] The law [72] does not mention abstinence; hence meat at the one full meal is allowed.[73]

When the vigil preceding the consecration of a church should fall on a Sunday or Feastday of obligation, authors are not agreed whether the fast must be observed. Beste writes: "Si pervigilia in diem dominicam vel festum de praecepto incidat, cessat obligatio ieiunandi ad tenorem can. 1252, § 4." [74] Maroto (+1937) stated: "Si dies, quae consecrationem praecedit, sit dominica vel festum de praecepto, tunc non urget seu cessat istiusmodi ieiunii obligatio, nimirum non est in aliam diem anticipandum ieiunium, quod rationem pervigilii induit (canon 1252, § 4)." [75]

Cappello holds the opposite view and writes: "Inde tamen minime sequitur cessare obligationem ieiunii, si consecratio habenda sit feria secunda vel postridie alicuius festi de praecepto. Hoc in casu aut in ipso pervigilio consecrationis ieiunium servandum est aut anticipandum in Sabbato seu die praecedenti . . . agitur quippe de obligatione *semel* tantum implenda." [76] Vermeersch-Creusen follow Cappello and write: "Et quia liturgia anticipat vigilias, ieiunium

[69] S. C. C., *Buscoducen.*, 3 iul. 1909—*Fontes*, VI, n. 4354; *AAS*, I (1909), 623-625.

[70] Augustine, *A Commentary on Canon Law*, VI, 23-24; Ayrinhac, *Administrative Legislation*, n. 14.

[71] *PCI*, 20 iul. 1929—*AAS*, XXI (1929), 573.

[72] Canon 1166, § 2.

[73] Ayrinhac, *Administrative Legislation*, n. 14; Beste, *Introductio in Codicem*, p. 560; cf. canon 1251.

[74] *Introductio in Codicem*, p. 560.

[75] "De ieiunio in consecratione ecclesiae"—*Apollinaris*, III (1930), 236-238.

[76] Cappello, "Annotationes, III"—*Periodica*, XVIII (1929), 253.

istud liturgicum servandum putamus in pervigilio festi post quod immediate fiat dedicatio." [77]

The *Pontifical Commission* for the Interpretation of the Code [78] decreed that the fast which is mentioned in canon 1166, § 2, is to be regulated according to the common law of ecclesiastical fast, hence canon 1252, § 4, is applicable, and if the vigil preceding the consecration of a church falls on a Sunday or a Feastday of obligation, it would seem that the fast does not have to be observed or anticipated.[79]

The obligation of fasting on the day preceding the consecration of a church which is prescribed by the Code [80] and the Roman Pontifical is not applicable when a church is dedicated by blessing, for the Code and the Roman Ritual do not prescribe the fast preceding the blessing of a church.

Article 5. Altars and the Consecration and Blessing of Churches

The relationship between the consecration of altars and the consecration of churches is indicated in the Roman Pontifical under three separate titles: *De ecclesiae dedicatione seu consecratione, De altaris consecratione quae fit sine ecclesiae dedicatione,* and *De altaris portatilis consecratione.*[81]

Canon 1165, § 5: Altare consecrari potest etiam sine ecclesiae consecratione; sed una simul cum ecclesia debet saltem altare maius consecrari aut altare secundarium, si maius sit iam consecratum.

The Code describes the relationship between the consecration of altars and the consecration of churches in canon 1165 § 5, by stating that an altar may be consecrated without the accompanying conse-

[77] Vermeersch-Creusen, *Epitome,* II, n. 483.

[78] 20 iul. 1929—*AAS,* XXI (1929), 573.

[79] The Congregation of the Council is competent to dispense from the fast. Cf. canon 250.

[80] Canon 1166, § 2.

[81] Cf. Bliley, *Altars,* pp. 85-88; pp. 106-107.

cration of a church, but that along with the consecration of a church at least the main altar must be consecrated, or if the main altar is already consecrated, some lesser altar in the same church must be consecrated.

An altar certainly may be consecrated without the accompanying consecration of a church,[82] but what is to be said about the consecration of a church without the accompanying consecration of an altar? The Roman Pontifical [83] includes the ceremonies for the consecration of an altar as an integral part of the ceremonies for the consecration of a church. The Sacred Congregation of Rites [84] gave several decisions to the effect that if a church were consecrated without the accompanying consecration of an altar, the consecration of the church would be valid but unlawful, unless an Apostolic dispensation were had. The entire order of ceremonies as found in the Roman Pontifical must be observed in order that the integrity of the consecration may be had.

What should be done if a church is to be consecrated, and all the altars are already consecrated? For the lawful consecration of the church without the accompanying consecration of an altar, an Apostolic dispensation should be obtained. Otherwise, authors [85] suggest that one of the altars be exsecrated and then consecrated anew, or else, if it be possible, there should be erected another altar which can be consecrated with the church. The general norm is that a church may not be consecrated lawfully if all the altars are already consecrated, so that none remains to be consecrated. The Sacred Congregation of Rites [86] decreed that it was not permitted to consecrate a church and simply to omit the ceremonies that pertain to the consecration of an altar.

[82] Canon 1165, § 5; Pontificale Romanum, Tit., *De altaris consecratione quae fit sine ecclesiae dedicatione.*

[83] Tit., *De ecclesiae dedicatione seu consecratione.*

[84] 19 sept. 1665, ad 2—*Decr. Auth.*, n. 1321; 28 sept. 1872—*Decr. Auth.*, n. 3286; 19 maii 1896, ad I—*Decr. Auth.*, n. 3907.

[85] Beste, *Introductio in Codicem,* p. 559; Coronata, *De Locis et Temporibus Sacris,* n. 21; Joannes Ferreres, *Institutiones Canonicae* (2. ed., 2 vols., Barcinone, 1920), II, n. 56; Gasparri, *De Ss. Eucharistia,* nn. 160-162; Vermeersch-Creusen, *Epitome,* II, n. 482.

[86] 3 martii 1866, ad I—*Decr. Auth.*, n. 3142.

In regard to the dedication of a church by blessing, neither the Code nor the Roman Ritual mentions the necessity of consecrating an altar when the church is being blessed.

In a consecrated church at least one altar, preferably the high altar, must be a fixed altar in the strict liturgical sense; but in churches that are only blessed, all the altars may be movable.[87] In a church all the altars may be consecrated as fixed altars, provided that they have been properly constructed according to the demands of the Code.[88]

The Sacred Congregation of Rites [89] declared that in every blessed church at least one quasi-fixed *(ad modum fixi)* altar should be constructed if the church did not contain a consecrated fixed altar. This quasi-fixed altar should have a stone foundation. In the altar a consecrated altar-stone was to be inserted; but all the other altars could be built of wood, to which, of course, had to be added the consecrated altar stone.[90] In every blessed church, therefore, if the high altar is not fixed in the strict liturgical sense, there should be a quasi-fixed high altar.

If several altars are to be consecrated in conjunction with the consecration of a church, it is not necessary that the consecrating bishop of the church also consecrate all the altars. The consecrating bishop of the church may reserve one altar which he consecrates in conjunction with the consecration of the church, while the other altars may be consecrated by other bishops. This seems to be the practice in Rome.[91]

Coronata,[92] following Many,[93] writes that certain parts of the consecration ceremonies of a church may be divided among several bishops. For example, one bishop may sprinkle the outside walls of the church, another bishop the inside walls. Benedict XIV (1740-

[87] Canon 1197, § 2.

[88] Cf. canons 1197-1202; Bliley, *Altars*, pp. 51-74.

[89] 31 aug. 1867, ad I—*Decr. Auth.*, n. 3162.

[90] Bliley, *Altars*, p. 77.

[91] Beste, *Introductio in Codicem*, p. 559; Vermeersch-Creusen, *Epitome*, II, n. 482.

[92] *De Locis et Temporibus Sacris*, n. 22, footnote 3.

[93] *De Locis Sacris*, n. 14.

1758) adduced many examples of this practice[94] and stated: ". . . non ab uno ergo tantum, sed a pluribus episcopis, eiusdem ecclesiae dedicatio fieri potest." [95]

Benedict XIV held that two bishops may divide the unction of the twelve crosses between each other in the consecration of a church, provided that one and the same bishop anoints some of the crosses and at the same time recites the form, in the same manner as among the Orientals several priests divide among themselves the unctions that are made in administering extreme unction to one person critically sick.[96]

When there is but one altar which is to be consecrated in conjunction with the consecration of a church, then it is not permitted to divide the ceremonial rites between two bishops, so that one bishop would consecrate the church, and the other bishop would consecrate the altar. This is forbidden by a decree of the Sacred Congregation of Rites.[97]

If for any reason the consecrating bishop is impeded in completing the ceremonies of the consecration of a church, then the bishop who continues the ceremonies must repeat all the ceremonies of consecration if the twelve crosses were not anointed by the former consecrating bishop. If the twelve crosses were anointed, and the bishop is impeded in finishing the ceremonies, then the bishop who continues the ceremonies does not repeat any of them up to and inclusive of the anointing of the twelve crosses, but continues with the ceremonies from that point forward.[98]

Article 6. Every Church to Have a Title

Canon 1168, § 1: Unaquaeque ecclesia consecrata vel benedicta suum habeat titulum; qui, peracta ecclesiae dedicatione, mutari nequit.

[94] In epistola *Peracta,* ad Abbatem Campidonensem, 16 nov. 1748, §§ 4-9—*Bullarium SSmi. Domini Nostri Benedicti XIV* (4. ed., 4 vols., Venice, 1778), III, Pars Secunda, pp. 451-456.

[95] *Ibid.,* § 10.

[96] *Ibid.,* §§ 10-17.

[97] 3 martii 1866, ad II—*Decr. Auth.,* n. 3142.

[98] Many, *De Locis Sacris,* n. 14.

In the same manner as an altar has its title, so also a church must have its proper title. Each church which is either consecrated or blessed shall have its title, which cannot be changed after the dedication of the church has been performed. The title is bestowed in the dedication of the church, for the Roman Pontifical and the Roman Ritual prescribe that the name or names be mentioned in several places in the ceremonies of dedication.[99]

A. *Meaning of the Title*

It is impossible to go into detail on the origin and meaning of the word *"titulus"* within the confines of this chapter. A short history of the various uses of the word *"titulus"* before its adoption by the Church into its official language will enable one to acquire a better understanding of the canonical concept as found in the Code.

The word *"titulus"* comes, according to Sextus Pompeius Festus, (fl. c. 300) [100] from *"tutulus"* (from *tuendo* or *tegendo*). Thus the soldiers of Rome who protected the homeland were called *"tituli,"* from which the proper name *Titus* arose. According to Marcus Terentius Varro (116-27 B. C.) [101] the term *"titulus"* was used to denote the higher portions of a city, the *arx* or citadel, which protected the city against attack. From this use another arose. The roof of a house was referred to as a *"titulus,"* and the goddess to whom the house was dedicated was given the name *"Tutelina."* [102]

Among the Romans it was the custom to place a stone, called a *"titulus,"* to mark the confines of property. On this stone was marked the name of the owner or his sign. This name or sign upon the stone, or an inscription or tablet on a house, was an expression of ownership by law.[103] This title was called *"titulus fiscalis"* and was used by the emperors to designate imperial property. Of a similar nature

[99] Cf. Pontificale Romanum, tit., *De ecclesiae dedicatione seu consecratione;* Rituale Romanum, tit. VIII, caput 27, *Ritus benedicendi novam ecclesiam seu oratorium publicum.*

[100] *De Verborum Significatione* (Romae, 1826), XVIII, 41.

[101] *De Lingua Latina* (Romae, 1821), VI, p. 68.

[102] Buonocore, *Il Titulus Canonicus* (2 vols., Napoli, 1933), I, 38.

[103] Hinschius, *Das Kirchenrecht der Katholiken und Protestanten in Deutschland* (6 vols., Berlin, 1869-1897), I, 63. Also c. 1, C. XVI, q. 6.

were the veils or "*vela cortina,*" titles of the emperors enscribed with the picture and the name of the emperor, as a sign of possession.

The Romans also used the word "*titulus*" to designate a small tablet or inscription which was hung upon the neck or placed above the head of criminals condemned to death, indicating the crime for which they were punished. It was such a title which was placed above the head of Christ on the cross: the title of *Rex Iudaeorum* in three languages, Aramaic, Greek, and Latin, stating the cause and reason for the death penalty.[104] For the martyrs who followed Christ and whose only crime was "quod christiani essent," the title with the reason of punishment was the one word "Christianus." [105] These were some of the meanings and uses of the word "*titulus*" before the Church incorporated this word into its official language. The original use and meaning of the word "*titulus*" by the Church is obscured by the mists of tradition. The first mention of the term as used in the Church occurs in the *Liber Pontificalis,* in its story of the life of Pope St. Evaristus (112-121), "Hic titulos in Urbe Roma divisit Presbyteris et Septem Diaconos Constituit." [106]

How the Church adapted the term "*titulus*" in its various uses and evolution throughout the centuries is a study beyond the scope of this dissertation. For the purpose in hand the word *title* can designate the church itself, or it can designate any sacred person or mystery under the protection of which a church is dedicated, and by which the church is known and distinguished from other churches in the same manner as in baptism a person receives a name by which he is distinguished from other persons.[107]

A distinction must be made between the title and the patron of a church. The title of a church may also be the patron of a church,

[104] John XIX, 19, 20; Matt. XXVII, 37; Mark XV, 26.

[105] Laemmer, *Eusebii Pamphili Historia Ecclesiastica,* pp. 327-353.

[106] Duchesne, *Liber Pontificalis,* I, 126.

[107] S. R. C., 9 maii 1857—*Decr. Auth.,* n. 3048; Beste, *Introductio in Codicem,* p. 560; Blat, *Commentarium,* III, n. 18; Coronata, *De Locis et Temporibus Sacris,* n. 24; Gasparri, *De Ss. Eucharistia,* I, n. 137; Many, *De Locis Sacris,* n. 20; Pego, "De Titularibus et Patronis"—*Ephemerides Liturgicae,* XXXIII (1919), 256; Vermeersch-Creusen, *Epitome,* II, n. 485; Wernz, *Ius Decretalium,* III, n. 439.

but this can be so only if the title is that of a person, *(persona creata, non increata)* as for example when there is question of a St. Mary's Church, a St. Gabriel's Church, or a St. Peter's Church. In these cases, the Blessed Virgin, St. Gabriel, and St. Peter are the titles of the churches and likewise the patrons of the respective churches. When the title of a church is an uncreated reality, as for example when one speaks of a Resurrection Church, we can only speak of the title of the church, and not the patron of the church. Since the patron is an advocate before God, only the Blessed Virgin, an Angel, Archangel, or Saint may be chosen; the Blessed Trinity, the Holy Ghost, or Our Divine Lord in any of His Mysteries, as the Nativity, Resurrection, Ascension, may not be chosen as the patron, but only as the title of a church.[108]

B. *Titles That May be Used*

The bishop chooses the title of a church,[109] although he may acquiesce to the desire of the patron or founder of a church. Gasparri [110] concedes the right of naming the title to the founder of the church.

The title is chosen at the laying of the corner stone; however, it is definitively and properly constituted at the consecration or blessing of the church,[111] and therefore the feast of the title of a church is not celebrated from the time of the laying of the corner stone, but from the day of the consecration or blessing. Between the time of the laying of the corner stone and the dedication of a church the bishop may change the title of a church. This is impossible without an Apostolic Indult once the church is dedicated.[112]

[108] Cf. authors cited in the preceding footnote.

[109] S. R. C., 21 apr. 1873, ad I—*Decr. Auth.*, n. 3296; Ayrinhac, *Administrative Legislation*, n. 15; Beste, *Introductio in Codicem*, p. 561; Coronata, *De Locis et Temporibus Sacris*, n. 24; *Ephemerides Liturgicae, ibid.*, p. 258, nn. 19-20.

[110] *De Ss. Eucharistia*, I, n. 137, footnote.

[111] Beste, *Introductio in Codicem*, p. 561; Coronata, *De Locis et Temporibus Sacris*, n. 24; *Ephemerides Liturgicae, ibid.*, p. 258, n. 20.

[112] S. R. C., 6 sept. 1834, ad 2—*Decr. Auth.*, n. 2719; S. R. C., 18 febr. 1843, ad I—*Decr. Auth.*, n. 2853.

Titles of churches may be:

1. The Blessed Trinity or one of the Divine Persons.

2. Any mystery or object which has relation to Our Lord, as the Incarnation or the Resurrection, or the Holy Cross or the Crown of Thorns.

3. The Blessed Virgin and her various prerogatives and special attributes.

4. The Angels, not only cumulatively, but likewise singly, as long as it is a name of an Angel venerated by name in the Church.

5. Saints whose names are found in the Martyrology.

6. The prerogatives, privileges, or special claims to honor in the lives of the Saints, expressed in such titles as the Chains of St. Peter, the Conversion of St. Paul, the Stigmata of St. Francis, etc.[113]

Ordinarily one title is chosen, but if the title has the names of two saints and they occur on different days in the liturgical calendar, the feast of each saint has to be kept on the respective days.[114]

If the title of a church is that of the Blessed Virgin, without the addition of a particular mystery or title, the titular feast is to be kept on the Feast of the Assumption of the Blessed Virgin.[115]

C. *Titles that May Not be Used*

Certain titles are essentially barred from use, while others may be employed only with the permission of the Holy See.

1. Churches cannot be dedicated to beatified persons without an indult of the Holy See.[116]

2. Churches cannot be dedicated to persons who have received only the title of Venerable from the Church.[117]

[113] Beste, *Introductio in Codicem*, p. 561; Coronata, *De Locis et Temporibus Sacris*, n. 24; *Ephemerides Liturgicae, ibid.*, p. 259, n. 21; Gasparri, *De Ss. Eucharistia*, I, n. 138; Many, *De Locis Sacris*, n. 21.

[114] S. R. C., 18 iunii 1885, ad VI—*Decr. Auth.*, n. 3637.

[115] S. R. C., 10 martii 1787—*Decr. Auth.*, n. 2529.

[116] Canon 1168, § 3. Ecclesiae dedicari Beatis nequeunt sine Sedis Apostolicae indulto.

[117] Gasparri, *De Ss. Eucharistia*, I, n. 138: "Vetitum est, sine apostolico indulto, quod difficile admodum conceditur, ecclesiam dedicare in honorem *Beatorum*, . . . et multo magis vetitum est ecclesiam dedicare in honorem *Venerabilium*."

3. New churches cannot be dedicated to Saints of the Old Testament.[118] Churches which have been consecrated centuries ago may retain the title of Saints of the Old Testament.

4. Before any new, unusual or strange title may be adopted, the bishop must consult the Sacred Congregation of Rites. This Congregation [119] forbade, for example, the title of "The Sacred Eucharistic Heart of Jesus" to be used in the sacred Liturgy inasmuch as it was neither canonical nor liturgical, and particularly because it savored of novelty.[120]

D. *Change of Title*

Canon 1168, § 1: Unaquaeque ecclesia consecrata vel benedicta suum habeat titulum; qui, peracta ecclesiae dedicatione, mutari nequit.

The title of a church cannot be changed after the dedication of the church has been executed. After the laying of the corner stone, at which a title is used, but before the dedication, the bishop may change the title. But once the dedication either by consecration or by blessing has taken place, the bishop of his own accord may not change the original title, but he needs an Apostolic Indult.[121]

Vermeersch-Creusen [122] assert that the words of canon 1168, § 1, "*. . . peracta ecclesiae dedicatione, mutari nequit ecclesiae titulus,*" refer only to the case of a consecration, and not to that of a blessing.

[118] S. R. C., 3 aug. 1697—*Decr. Auth.*, n. 1978.

[119] 28 martii 1914, ad III—*AAS*, VI (1914), 383.

[120] For other details in the above matter, the following liturgists may be consulted: Joannes Cavalieri, *Opera Omnia Liturgica, Seu Commentaria* (Quinque Tomis Comprehensa Venetiis, 1758), Tom. 1, Cap. II, pp. 45-78; P. J. B. De Herdt, *Sacrae Liturgiae Praxis* (3 vols., Louvanii, 1889), III, nn. 118-125; J. F. Van Der Stappen, *Sacra Liturgia* (5 vols., Mechliniae, 1900-1904), I, pp. 380-410; Innocentius Wapelhorst, *Compendium Sacrae Liturgiae* (11. ed., Benziger Brothers, New York, 1931), nn. 339-342; Joseph Wuest-Thomas W. Mullaney, *Matters Liturgical* (4. ed., Frederick Pustet, New York, 1934), nn. 726-733.

[121] S. R. C., 6 sept. 1834, ad 2—*Decr. Auth.*, n. 2719; S. R. C., 12 sept 1857, ad 14—*Decr. Auth.*, n. 3059.

[122] *Epitome*, II, n. 485.

For their statement they rely on the interpretation which obtained antecedently to the Code when the word "dedication" had to be understood strictly in the sense of a consecration only. Coronata [123] writes: "Titulus, peracta ecclesiae dedicatione, mutari nequit (c. 1168, § 1). Quod valet non solum de dedicatione sollemni sed et de dedicatione simplici seu benedictione," but Vermeersch-Creusen [124] assert that Coronata does not offer any reason for substantiating his view.

Blat [125] writes: *"peracta Ecclesiae dedicatione per alterutrum sacramentale* [by consecration or by blessing], *mutari nequit,* [*titulus*] *nempe: ab inferioribus Praelatis."*

Beste [126] considers it to be a more probable opinion that the title cannot be changed after the church has been dedicated by blessing. "Titulus mutari nequit post peractam consecrationem; num idem etiam dicendum sit de dedicatione per benedictionem, disputatur, probabilius autem affirmandum est." Ayrinhac [127] also regards it as a more probable opinion that the title cannot be changed after the church has been dedicated by blessing, except by the Holy See, but for his statement he points to no specific reason. According to norms given in canon 18 and applied to canon 1168, § 1, the writer asserts that the title of a church cannot be changed except by the Holy See, once the church has been dedicated either by consecration or by blessing.

The writer agrees indeed with Vermeersch-Creusen that the word "dedication," according to pre-Code interpretation, was in strict parlance understood in the sense of consecration. But of course the text and context has to be taken into consideration when one reads the pre-Code authors, for at times the word "dedication" was used also in the sense of dedicating a church by blessing, and hence it cannot be affirmed absolutely that the word "dedication" always meant consecration.

It is the present text and context of canon 1168, § 1, that calls

123 *De Locis et Temporibus Sacris,* n. 24.

124 *Epitome,* II, n. 485, p. 334, footnote 1.

125 *Commentarium,* III, n. 18.

126 *Introductio in Codicem,* p. 561.

127 *Administrative Legislation,* n. 15.

for investigation and interpretation. That canon reads: "Unaquaeque ecclesia *consecrata* vel *benedicta* suum habeat titulum; qui, peracta ecclesiae dedicatione, mutari nequit." Every church that is *consecrated* or *blessed* must have a title. In compliance with the first clause of canon 1168, § 1, a *consecrated* church will have a title and a *blessed* church will have a title. The second clause of canon 1168, § 1, states: *"qui,* peracta ecclesiae dedicatione, mutari nequit." The pronoun *"qui"* refers to *"titulum"* of the preceding clause, in which it is stated that a *consecrated* or *blessed* church must have a title. If, as Vermeersch-Creusen assert, the word "dedication" in the clause, "qui, peracta ecclesiae *dedicatione,* mutari nequit," is to denote only *consecration,* then the legislator would in all probability have expressly used the word *"consecration,"* because the Code carefully distinguishes the words "dedication," "consecration," and "blessing" in the canons where these words are used. The preceding canon (1167) states: "Festum *consecrationis* ecclesiae quotannis celebretur ad normam legum liturgicarum." The Code does not use the word *"dedicationis"* in that canon, for that would imply that the feast of the consecration and the feast of the blessing of a church would have to be celebrated annually. To exclude the necessity of celebrating the feast of a blessed church, the Code does not employ the word *"dedicationis,"* which could be interpreted to mean the dedication of a church by blessing. To avoid all misunderstanding the word *"consecrationis"* is employed. The natural interpretation, therefore, of canon 1168, § 1, is that the title of a church that has been dedicated, either by consecration or by blessing, cannot be changed once the church has been dedicated either by consecration or by blessing. But if a church had been utterly destroyed, or if it had collapsed and later was being rebuilt, then the title could be changed by the bishop at the time of dedication.[128]

When a church by the authority of the local ordinary is diverted from its sacred use by being reduced to a secular use because of the

[128] S. R. C., 29 martii 1760—*Decr. Auth.,* n. 2453; S. R. C., 16 ian. 1885—*Decr. Auth.,* n. 3625; S. R. C., 11 martii 1843—*Decr. Auth.,* n. 2853. Cf. also Beste, *Introductio in Codicem,* p. 561; Coronata, *De Locis et Temporibus Sacris,* n. 24; Vermeersch-Creusen, *Epitome,* II, n. 485.

fact that the church is dilapidated, and all means to repair it are wanting, then the local ordinary shall, if there is question of a parochial church, transfer its title to some other church.[129]

[129] Cf. canon 1187.

CHAPTER VIII

THE MINISTER OF THE CONSECRATION AND BLESSING OF A CHURCH

Section I. The Minister of Consecration

THUS far there has been discussed both the necessity for and obligation of consecrating or blessing churches as contained in the ancient and present discipline of the Church. A classification of the various types of churches that are to be consecrated or blessed was given. Finally, there were indicated the canonical requirements to be fulfilled relative to the church building proper before it may be consecrated or blessed.

The consideration of the present chapter will be concerned with the minister for valid and lawful consecration and blessing of churches. For the purpose of clarity, the chapter is divided into two sections, the first dealing with the minister of consecration, and the second with the minister of blessing. In the study of these two sections, it will appear who is the minister for the valid and lawful dedication of churches.

ARTICLE 1. THE NATURE AND ORIGIN OF THE POWER OF CONSECRATING CHURCHES

The Code gives the following rule relative to consecrations:

Canon 1147, § 1: "Consecrationes nemo qui charactere episcopali careat, valide peragere potest, nisi vel iure vel apostolico indulto id ei permittatur."

Canonists are in agreement that the rite of consecrating and of blessing churches has been instituted by the Church, and that the consecration of a church is an act of the power of the episcopal order.

The power of orders may derive from a twofold source: (1) the divine law, and (2) the ecclesiastical law.[1] The consecrating of churches is an act of the power of orders deriving from the ecclesiastical law and not from the divine law, for the act of consecrating churches is of purely ecclesiastical origin. The consecrating of churches, like acts of consecration in general, is reserved to those who have the episcopal character.[2]

Pirhing (+1679) taught:

> "Nec potest Episcopus delegare potestatem consecrandi ecclesias alteri simplici presbytero, Sive non Episcopo, cum ea potestas non sit iurisdictionis, sed ordinis episcopalis." [3]

Schmalzgrueber (+1735) stated:

> "Consecratio ecclesiae . . . est actus ordini episcopali soli adnexus." [4]

Santi (+1885) explained:

> "Ritus consecrationis ecclesiae institutus est ad imitationem sacramenti ordinis. Hinc consecratio dicitur esse actus ordinis, at eo sensu quia ex institutione Ecclesiae sacer minister dedicans cultui divino locum imitatur consecrationem personae in sacra ordinatione." [5]

Wernz (+1914) simply asserted: "Consecratio ecclesiae est actus ordinis episcopalis." [6] Many (+1922) declared: "Minister ordinarius consecrationis ecclesiarum est Episcopus . . . Under deducitur theoria

[1] Beste, *Introductio in Codicem*, p. 222; Gasparri, *De Sacra Ordinatione* (2 vols., Parisiis, 1893-1894), n. 1138; Vermeersch-Creusen, *Epitome*, I, n. 323; Wernz-Vidal, *Ius Canonicum*, II, 376.

[2] Canon 1147, § 1.

[3] *Jus Canonicum Nova Methodo Explicatum* (5 vols in 4, Dilingae, 1674-1678), lib. III, tit. 40, n. 1.

[4] *Ius ecclesiasticum universum*, lib. III, tit. 40, n. 15.

[5] *Praelectiones Juris Canonici* (2 vols., Ratisbonae, Neo-Eboraci, Cincinnati, 1886), lib. III, tit. 40, n. 1.

[6] *Ius Decretalium*, III, n. 437.

canonica, nempe Ecclesiam quae ritum illum propria actoritate instituit, eumdem annexuisse ordini episcopali, sicut Christus ipse plura ex institutis a se sacramentis eidem ordini episcopali annexuit." [7]

Gasparri (+1934) wrote: "Consecratio est actus ordinis episcopalis, quem simplici sacerdoti unus Romanus Pontifex committere potest. Romanus Pontifex potest quoque ratam habere altaris vel ecclesiae consecrationem quae nulla fuit, cum versemur in materia mere ecclesiastica." [8] From the teaching of these canonists, it is evident that the consecration of churches is to be regarded as an act of the power of orders deriving from ecclesiastical law, which power is annexed by the positive wish of the Church to the episcopal order. The consecration of churches is not an act of the power of jurisdiction, for any consecration performed by one who is endowed with the episcopal order is always valid, but may for various reasons not always be lawful.[9] This will be more fully shown in the discussion regarding the validity of a consecration by an excommunicated, suspended, heretical, deposted or degraded bishop.

The Code mentions two other sources besides the episcopal character as furnishing the power whereby consecrations may be validly effected:

> "Consecrationes nemo qui charactere episcopali careat, valide peragere potest, nisi vel iure vel apostolico indulto id ei permittatur." [10]

In order, then, that a minister may validly consecrate a church, the power of consecrating must be had from one or the other of three sources: (1) episcopal consecration; (2) qualification by law, or (3) authorization by apostolic indult. To simplify the consideration of who may be constituted as a minister for the valid consecration of a church, the following schema is proposed.

[7] *De Locis Sacris*, n. 11.

[8] *De Ss. Eucharistia*, I, n. 156.

[9] Cf. canon 1147, § 1; Maroto, "De ecclesiae consecratione,"—*Apollinaris*, IV (1931), 247.

[10] Canon 1147, § 1.

The act of consecrating a church may be performed

- I. in virtue of the episcopal character (*consecratio episcopalis*)
  1. by residential bishops
  2. by titular bishops
     - a. coadjutors
     - b. auxiliaries
- II. in virtue of their ecclesiastical office (*potestas a iure*)
  1. by cardinals
  2. by abbots and prelates who as ordinaries exercise territorial jurisdiction
- III. in consequence of a delegated authorization (*facultas ex apostolico indulto*)
  1. by a vicar or prefect apostolic
  2. by an apostolic administrator
  3. by a vicar capitular (or a diocesan administrator)
  4. by a vicar general of a residential bishop
  5. by a vicar general of an abbot or prelate who as an ordinary exercises territorial jurisdiction
  6. by a pro-vicar or pro-prefect apostolic
  7. by a priest or a cleric in major or minor orders
  8. by a layman

Article 2. The Minister of the Consecration of Churches *Ratione Consecrationis Episcopalis*

The general law of the Code relative to consecrations is expressed in canon 1147, § 1, which states that consecrations cannot be *validly* performed by one lacking the episcopal character, unless the faculty is given by law or by an apostolic indult. The essential requisite, as contemplated by the Code, for being constituted the ordinary minister for the valid consecration of a church, is that the minister possess the episcopal character, which is acquired in virtue of episcopal consecration.

A. *Residential Bishops*

Residential bishops are the ordinary and immediate pastors in the diocese entrusted to them.[11] The residential bishop-elect cannot take over the government of the diocese either in person or through others, or under any title, until he has taken canonical possession of his diocese. Canonical possession of the diocese is taken as soon as the bishop exhibits to the cathedral chapter in person or by proxy the apostolic papers of appointment, in the presence of the secretary of the chapter, or of the chancellor of the curia, who shall make entry of the fact in the acts of the diocese.[12] If the bishop-elect has not taken canonical possession of the diocese, then the right of consecrating churches in the diocese still vests in the ecclesiastical person who lawfully rules the diocese. If the latter person lacks the episcopal character, he has the right to call in a bishop to perform the consecration. He also is the one whom exempt religious have to petition if they desire to have their churches consecrated.[13]

The consecration of a place (church) presupposes, for validity, the power of the episcopal order,[14] and, for lawfulness, the power of properly authorized ecclesiastical jurisdiction.[15] The bishop cannot delegate his episcopal character, but he may delegate the power of

[11] Canon 334, § 1.

[12] Canon 334, § 2, § 3.

[13] Canons 1155 and 1157.

[14] Canon 1147, § 1.

[15] Cf. canons 1155, § 1, and 1157.

jurisdiction. Thus he is enabled to call a bishop into his territory to consecrate a church.[16]

The consecration of any place, though it belong to regulars pertains to the bishop of the territory in which such a place is situated. And even if the ordinary of the territory lacks the episcopal character, the providing for the consecration of a place is still his prerogative, for he has the right to call upon any bishop of the same rite to perform the consecration in his territory.[17]

The right or the prerogative of the ordinary of the territory to provide for the consecration of places within his territory embraces also the consecration of places that belong to regulars, so that, even though the ordinary of the territory is not a consecrated bishop, the regulars need his consent for the consecration of their places, even if their own religious superior is a bishop.[18]

Pre-Code law [19] clearly indicated that, even though a bishop built a church at his own expense in another diocese, he could not *lawfully* consecrate the church, but had to obtain permission from the bishop in whose territory the church was located. Regulars had to petition the local ordinary to have their churches consecrated.

When the ordinary of a territory lacks the episcopal character, he may give permission to any bishop of his own rite to perform consecrations in his territory.

Canon 1155, § 2: "Ordinarius territorii, licet charactere episcopali careat, potest cuilibet eiusdem ritus Episcopo licentiam dare consecrationes peragendi in suo territorio."

[16] Canon 1155.

[17] Canon 1155.

[18] Canons 1155 and 1157. "Haec est ratio, cur regulares, salvo contrario privilegio, recurrere debeant ad ordinarium loci ad petendas consecrationes locorum suorum, etsi superior ordinis regularis, ad quem locus pertinet, sit episcopus. . . . Sede vacante ius consecrationis transit ad vicarium capitularem, qui, si careat ordine episcopali, debet alium ministrum consecrationis designare et arcessere ad consecranda loca, *etiam regularium,* sui territorii."—Beste, *Introductio in Codicem,* p. 553.

[19] C. 28, C. VII, q. 1; c. 10, C. XVI, q. 1; c. 1, 3, C. XVI, q. 5; c. 1, X, *de religiosis domibus, ut episcopo sint subiectae,* III, 36.

Canon 1155, § 2, bars the use of any rite alien to that of the local ordinary who in law is given the prerogative to provide for the consecration of the church in his territory. The right of those whose church is to be consecrated determines the rite which must be used in the act of consecration. Hence a bishop of an Oriental rite may not consecrate a church that is to be used by the faithful of the Latin rite, or vice versa. The consecration of a church for the use of the faithful of the Latin rite by a bishop of the Oriental rite is nevertheless a valid act of consecration.[20]

1. Capacity for Delegating the Power to Bless Churches

Blessings are either reserved or not reserved.[21] The Index of the Roman Ritual gives a list of both classes. Among the reserved blessings some are reserved to the Pope, some to the local ordinary, some to certain religious superiors, and some to priests who have an apostolic indult. The Code decrees that the blessing of places which belong to the secular clergy or to non-exempt religious, or to lay persons, is reserved to the local ordinary in whose territory the place is situated.[22] The blessing of places which belong to exempt clerical religious is reserved to the major religious superior.[23] Canon 1147, § 2 decrees:

> "Benedictiones autem impertire potest quilibet presbyter, exceptis iis quae Romano Pontifici aut Episcopis aliisve reserventur."

The blessing of a church, although in itself a function of the priestly order by ecclesiastical right is reserved to the local ordinary in whose territory the church is situated, or to the major religious superior if the church belongs to exempt clerical religious.[24] Canon 1156 reserves the right of blessing a place either to the local ordinary or to the major religious superior and canon 1157 demands the consent

[20] Canon 1147, § 1; Beste, *Introductio in Codicem*, p. 554.

[21] Cf. Canon 1147, § 2.

[22] Cf. Canon 1156.

[23] Canon 1156.

[24] Augustine, *Commentary on Canon Law*, IV, pp. 563-564; Coronata, *De Locis et Temporibus Sacris*, n. 5; Vermeersch-Creusen, *Epitome*, II, n. 465.

of the proper ordinary before a place can be blessed, but both canons do not have an invalidating clause added. If a priest does not obtain the necessary delegation and blesses a church, the act would be valid, but unlawful. Thus canon 1147, § 3 decrees:

> "Benedictio reservata quae a presbytero detur sine necessaria licentia, illicita est, sed valida, nisi in reservatione Sedes Apostolica aliud expresserit."

The Sacred Congregation of Rites decreed that bishops are not permitted to grant faculties to priests to impart all the blessings that are classified as reserved in the Roman Ritual and in which blessings no anointment is used since that would exceed the ordinary or customary power of the bishops.[25] No difficulty exists about the capacity for delegating the power to bless churches which is reserved either to the local ordinary, or to the major religious superior for a church that belongs to exempt religious. The Code in canon 1156 states that the local ordinary and the religious superior may delegate a priest to perform the blessing. This is an express instance where the law permits the delegation of the reserved blessing of a place to a priest. The reservation of the blessing of a place is not explicitly accompanied by an *invalidating* clause; and hence, if a priest blessed a church without the necessary delegation, the act would be valid but unlawful.[26] The act of blessing a church by one lacking the priestly order would be invalid since, by ecclesiastical sanction, blessings are reserved to the priestly order.[27] The local ordinary or religious superior may delegate only a priest to bless a church, " . . . uterque vero potest alium *sacerdotem* ad hoc delegare." [28] A deacon, subdeacon, cleric in minor orders, or a layman could not be delegated by the local ordinary or religious superior to bless a church because the local ordinary and religious superior cannot delegate the power of priestly order.[29] Since the blessing of places is of ecclesiastical origin and attached by the positive disposition of the Church to the

[25] S. R. C., 2 apr. 1875—*Decr. Auth.*, n. 3343.

[26] Cf. canon 1147, § 3 and canon 1157.

[27] Cf. canon 1147, § 2.

[28] Canon 1156.

[29] Cf. canon 210.

priestly order for the validity of the act, the Supreme Pontiff alone may delegate a person who lacks the priestly order to validly bless a sacred place. The above point will be treated more fully in Section II, Articles 1 and 2, of this Chapter.

A distinction worthy of mention here is that the vicar general is not excluded by canon 1156 from the capacity of delegating the power to bless churches, while in canon 1155, § 1, the *consecration* of a place [a church] is one of those affairs in which the vicar general, even though he is a bishop, lacks competence and, therefore, needs a special mandate from the local ordinary.

2. Lack of Capacity for Delegating the Power to Consecrate Churches

It was the common and certain teaching of pre-Code authors [30] that a bishop could not delegate the power of orders, and hence the authors also mentioned that a bishop could not delegate any one who lacked the episcopal character to consecrate churches. This power of delegation they recognized as an exclusive prerogative of the Supreme Pontiff.

This doctrine that the bishop cannot delegate the power of orders is affirmed in the Code: "Potestas ordinis, a legitimo Superiore ecclesiastico sive adnexa officio sive commissa personae, nequit aliis demandari, nisi id expresse fuerit iure vel indulto concessum." [31] Nowhere in the Code does one find given to bishops the right which permits them to delegate anyone who lacks the episcopal character to consecrate churches, which act connotes a power proper to the episcopal order. On the contrary, the Code declares that no one who lacks the episcopal character can validly perform consecrations, unless the law permits it, or an apostolic indult has been obtained.[32] Hence the bishop cannot delegate the power of consecrating churches to anyone who lacks episcopal consecration.

[30] Gasparri, *De Ss. Eucharistia,* I, n. 156; Many, *De Locis Sacris,* n. 11; Schmalzgrueber, *Ius Ecclesiasticum Universum,* lib. III, tit. 40, n. 15; Wernz, *Ius Decretalium,* III, n. 437.

[31] Canon 210.

[32] Canon 1147, § 1. Consecrationes nemo qui charactere episcopali careat, valide peragere potest, nisi vel iure vel apostolico indulto id ei permittatur.

B. *Titular Bishops (Coadjutor and Auxiliary Bishops)*

In the history of the early Church, and particularly at the time of the Mohammedan invasions, there are numerous accounts of bishops being expelled from their sees by the infidels. These bishops retained the title of their diocese, although they often lacked people or churches. Successors were also appointed to these dioceses, although they could not even hope to visit such dioceses. The Popes have continued to the present day to fill those ancient episcopal sees, thereby preserving the glorious memory of those dioceses, and thus conferring the episcopal dignity without its burdens upon ecclesiastics whom the Roman Pontiff honors in various capacities.[33]

Titular bishops are bishops in the full sense of the term, possessing the same power of orders as residential bishops, but they do not exercise any jurisdiction in their dioceses and do not even take possession of them.[34] By reason of episcopal consecration titular bishops are proper ministers for the valid consecration of churches.[35] To lawfully consecrate a church, the titular bishop needs the consent of the local ordinary in whose territory the church is located.[36] Without this consent of the local ordinary, the consecration of the church performed by a titular bishop would always be valid but unlawful.

The Roman Pontiff alone can assign to a bishop a coadjutor or auxiliary bishop. A coadjutor is usually assigned to the bishop personally, with the right of succession; sometimes, however, the coadjutor is given to the episcopal see. A coadjutor assigned to the person of the bishop without the right of succession is called by the special name of auxiliary bishop.[37]

The rights of coadjutor and auxiliary bishops are delineated in canons 351-355, and normally are further determined in the apostolic

[33] Thomassinus, *Vetus et Nova Ecclesiae Disciplina circa Beneficia et Beneficiarios* (Magontiaci, 1787), P. I. L. I, cc. 27, 28; Wernz, *Ius Decretalium,* II, n. 808.

[34] Canons 348 and 349.

[35] Canon 1147, § 1.

[36] Canons 1155 and 1157.

[37] Canon 350. For the origin and history of coadjutor and auxiliary bishops, cf. Thomassinus, *Vetus et Nova Ecclesiae Disciplina circa Beneficia et Beneficiarios,* P. II. L. II, cc. 55-59; Wernz, *Ius Decretalium,* II, n. 809.

letters of appointment. By reason of the episcopal consecration coadjutor and auxiliary bishops can validly consecrate any place. For the lawfulness of the act of consecration, canons 1155 and 1157 must be observed.

Article 3. The Minister of the Consecration of Churches *"ratione officii" (ex ipso iure)*

Besides those who have the right to consecrate a place validly in view of their episcopal character, the Code [38] grants the right of validly consecrating a place to persons who possess a certain ecclesiastical dignity or office, but who lack the episcopal character. This power *ex iure* for the consecrating of a place is, as will be seen, limited at times to a definite territory. Hence, if the act of consecrating a a place is exercised outside of the definite territory, the act is invalid.

A. *Cardinals*

The sacred college of cardinals is divided into three orders: the episcopal order, which includes only six cardinal bishops appointed to the suburbicarian sees; the presbyteral order, consisting of fifty cardinal priests; and the diaconal order, consisting of fourteen cardinal deacons.[39] Of course if a cardinal has the episcopal character, he may consecrate any place validly *ratione consecrationis episcopalis*. Under the present law, cardinals must be at least priests.[40]

All cardinals from the time of their promotion in consistory have the faculty anywhere to bless and consecrate churches, altars and sacred vessels, to bless abbots, and to perform similar functions excepting the consecration of the holy oils, if the cardinal is not a bishop. The various requisites of the law must of course be observed, and due regard must be had for canon 1157,[41] which rules that the

[38] Canon 1147, § 1.

[39] Canon 231.

[40] Canon 232, § 1.

[41] Canon 239, § 1, n. 20. Praeter alia privilegia quae in hoc Codice suis in titulis enumerantur, Cardinales omnes a sua promotione in Consistorio facultate gaudent: Consecrationes et benedictiones ecclesiarum, altarium, sacrae supellectilis, Abbatum aliasve similes, excepta oleorum sacrorum consecratione, si Cardinalis charactere episcopali careat, ubique locorum, servatis servandis, peragendi, firmo praescripto canon 1157.

consent of the ordinary is always required for the blessing or consecration of a sacred place. Cardinals do not have to comply with the regulation of canon 1157, that is, seek the consent of the ordinary when they consecrate a church or altar of their title, since canon 1155, § 1, gives cardinals this privilege: "Consecratio alicuius loci . . . spectat ad Ordinarium territorii in quo locus ipse reperitur . . . firmo iure S. R. E. Cardinalium consecrandi ecclesiam et altaria sui tituli." [42]

Outside of the case when a cardinal does not consecrate a church or altar of his title, he must observe canons 1155, § 1, and 1157 only for the lawfulness of the act. If a cardinal consecrates a church other than the church of his title without the consent of the local ordinary, the consecration is always valid but unlawful, for *ex iure* [43] all cardinals have the power of consecrating churches anywhere.

Augustine [44] writes: "Cardinals who are endowed with the episcopal character may, in virtue of a special privilege, consecrate churches and altars everywhere with the consent of the local ordinary." Coronata [45] declares: "Minister validae et licitae consecrationis est: Cardinales S. R. E. licet non Episcopi pro ecclesiis et altaribus sui tituli; etiam extra proprios titulos de licentia tamen Ordinarii, si episcopali character insigniti sint." Both Augustine and Coronata erroneously imply that a cardinal who is not a bishop cannot consecrate a church besides the church of his title. It is true that the act of consecration is proper to the power of the episcopal order, nevertheless, the power to consecrate a church derives merely from ecclesiastical law, as was explained.[46] The general law or the Roman Pontiff, and he alone, can grant to persons who are not endowed with the episcopal character the faculty of consecrating places and things.[47] All cardinals, even those who lack the episcopal character, may in virtue of the law [48] consecrate churches and altars everywhere with the consent

[42] Canon 1155, § 1.
[43] Canon 239, § 1, n. 20.
[44] *A Commentary on Canon Law*, VI, 4.
[45] *De Locis et Temporibus Sacris*, n. 5.
[46] Chapter VIII, Section I, Art. 1, pp. 78-81.
[47] Canon 1147, § 1.
[48] Canon 239, § 1, n. 20.

of the local ordinary. The law does prohibit cardinals from consecrating the holy oils, if the cardinals lack the episcopal character, but it does not prohibit cardinals from consecrating churches everywhere if the cardinals lack the episcopal character.

B. *Abbots and Prelates "Nullius"*

Abbots and prelates who are territorial ordinaries have the same ordinary powers and the same obligations with the same sanctions as a residential bishop in his diocese. If such an abbot or prelate does not possess the episcopal consecration, but has received whatever blessing he is bound by the law to receive, he has, besides the faculties mentioned in canon 294, § 2, the power to consecrate churches and immovable altars.[49]

An abbot or prelate who is endowed with territorial jurisdiction is a local ordinary in his territory,[50] and even though he lack the episcopal character he may, *ratione officii, ex ipso iure,* validly and lawfully consecrate churches within his territory.[51]

Augustine [52] erroneously writes that an abbot or prelate with territorial jurisdiction must call upon another bishop of the same rite to consecrate a place in his own territory if he lacks episcopal consecration. The Code in canon 323, § 2,[53] gives such an abbot or prelate the right to consecrate a church in his territory, even if he lacks the episcopal character. Before the Code, this right was not within his possession.[54]

A controversy existed before 1931 whether an abbot or prelate with territorial jurisdiction, but without the episcopal character, could validly consecrate a church outside his territory with the permission of the ordinary of the respective territory. The reason for

49 Canon 323.

50 Canon 198, § 2.

51 Canon 323, § 2.

52 *A Commentary on Canon Law,* VI, 4.

53 "Si charactere episcopali non sit ornatus et benedictionem, si eam recipere debet, receperit, praeter alia munera quae in canon 294, § 2, describuntur, potest quoque ecclesias et altaria immobilia consecrare."

54 Cappello, "De consecratione ecclesiarum,"—*Periodica,* XIX (1930), 135.

the controversy was based on canon 323, § 2, which grants such an abbot or prelate the faculty of consecrating churches and immovable altars, without invoking the restrictive clause, "intra sui territorii fines ac perdurante munere," which is found in canon 294, § 2, relative to vicars and prefects apostolic. It was concluded that the faculty of consecrating churches and immovable altars as possessed by the abbot or prelate in virtue of canon 323, § 2, was for its use not limited to their own territory, but was absolute and universal in the sense that he could validly consecrate churches and immovable altars everywhere, even outside of his own territory.

Cappello,[55] according to the rules of canon 18, from the text and context of canons 294, § 2, and 323, § 2, and also from parallel passages in the Code, clearly demonstrated that an abbot or prelate with territorial jurisdiction could not validly consecrate churches outside of his territory even with the permission of the ordinary of that territory solely in virtue of canon 323, § 2.

In 1931 the *Pontifical Commission* for the interpretation of the Code was asked: "Whether, in virtue of canon 323 an abbot *nullius* who has not the episcopal character can validly consecrate a church in another's territory, with the permission of the Ordinary of that territory. Reply: In the negative." [56]

To validly consecrate a church outside their territory, abbots and prelates with territorial jurisdiction need the episcopal character, or an apostolic indult.[57] Within their territory, even lacking the episcopal character, "perdurante munere" if they have received the requisite blessing, they can consecrate churches or fixed altars.[58]

[55] "De consecratione ecclesiarum,"—*Periodica,* XIX (1930), 139-142.

[56] Bouscaren, *Canon Law Digest,* I, 194; *AAS,* XXIII (1931), 110; Ayrinhac in 1930 wrote: "Abbots and Prelates *Nullius,* once they have received the blessing may consecrate churches and fixed altars within their territory and also outside of it with the consent of the local Ordinary." *Administrative Legislation,* n. 2. In view of the *Code Commission's* response of Jan. 29, 1931, Ayrinhac's statement must be corrected.

[57] Canon 1147, § 1.

[58] Cf. canon 323, § 2. For an excellent study on the abbot *nullius* in relation to the consecration of churches, the reader is referred to: Maroto, "De ecclesiae consecratione,"—*Apollinaris,* IV (1931), 243-250.

ARTICLE 4. THE MINISTER OF THE CONSECRATION OF CHURCHES *"Ratione Delegationis"*

Up to this point, consideration has been given not only to the minister who validly can consecrate a church by reason of his episcopal orders and also to the minister who can do so, even in the absence of the episcopal character, in virtue of holding a specific office with which the law connects the faculty of consecrating a church. There remains now to be considered the minister who is authorized validly to consecrate a church in consequence of a special faculty delegated by him by means of an apostolic indult.

A. *Vicar and Prefect Apostolic*

A vicar or prefect apostolic enjoys the same rights and faculties in his territory as a residential bishop, unless the Holy See has withheld such a right or faculty from him.[59]

If the vicar or prefect apostolic is not a consecrated bishop, he may not consecrate churches in his territory,[60] for he lacks the necessary episcopal character, and he has not the right in consequence of his office since the Code does not accord him that right. The words, "omnes benedictiones Episcopis reservatas," of canon 294, § 2, do not imply for a vicar or prefect apostolic the right to *consecrate* a church if he lacks the episcopal character.[61] The canon uses the word *"benedictiones,"* not *"consecrationes."* The only other possibility in virtue of which a vicar or prefect apostolic can validly consecrate churches in his territory is that he have received that right in his letter of appointment, or by special apostolic indult, namely *ratione delegationis*.

[59] Canon 294, § 1.

[60] Cf. canon 1147, § 1. Augustine claims that the vicar or prefect apostolic who lacks the episcopal character may consecrate churches in his territory.—*A Commentary on Canon Law*, II, 311-312. But other authors deny the right of a vicar or prefect apostolic to consecrate churches if he lacks the episcopal character. Cf. Ayrinhac, *Constitution of the Church in the New Code of Canon Law* (London; New York; Toronto: Longmans, Green & Co., 1930), n. 97; Beste, *Introductio in Codicem*, p. 256; Jone, *Gesetzbuch des kanonischen Rechtes*, I, 260; Vermeersch-Creusen, *Epitome*, I, n. 406.

[61] Cf. preceding footnote.

The vicar or prefect apostolic is a local ordinary in his territory.[62] Hence no one else can consecrate a place in his territory, even one that belongs to exempt religious, without his consent.[63] The vicar or prefect apostolic who lacks the episcopal character, or who is without an apostolic indult, may call in any bishop of the same rite to consecrate places in his territory.[64] It is evident that, if the vicar or prefect apostolic is a consecrated bishop, he can validly consecrate churches whether within or outside of his territory. But, if he consecrates a place outside of his territory, then the consent of the particular local ordinary is needed for the lawfulness of his act.

B. *Apostolic Administrator*

For the origin and history of the apostolic administrator the reader is referred to authors who have treated that question explicitly.[65]

The Supreme Pontiff, for grave and special reasons, sometimes entrusts the ruling of a canonically established diocese, either *plena sede,* or *vacante sede,* to an apostolic administrator, either permanently or for a certain length of time.[66] The rights, duties, and privileges of the apostolic administrator are to be judged from his letter of appointment, or, if the letter does not expressly state otherwise, his faculties are to be determined by canons 315-318, which deal with the apostolic administrator.[67]

An apostolic administrator who is endowed with the episcopal character may in virtue of his episcopal status validly consecrate churches in the territory which is committed to his administration. Outside of his territory, if he be endowed with the episcopal character, the apostolic administrator needs, for the lawfulness of his

[62] Canon 198, § 2.

[63] Canon 1157.

[64] Canon 1155, § 2.

[65] McDonough, *Apostolic Administrators,* The Catholic University of America Canon Law Studies, n. 139 (Washington, D. C.: The Catholic University of America Press, 1941), pp. 1-63; Wernz, *Ius Decretalium,* II, n. 704.

[66] Cf. canon 312.

[67] Canon 314.

act, only the consent of the local ordinary in whose territory the consecration of a place is to be performed.[68]

If the apostolic administrator lacks the episcopal consecration he may not validly consecrate churches in his territory, unless the right is given to him in his letters of appointment, or by means of an apostolic indult. The Code does not grant the faculty to consecrate churches to the office of an apostolic administrator when he lacks the episcopal consecration.[69]

Like the vicar or prefect apostolic, the apostolic administrator is a local ordinary.[70] Hence no one may, that is, no one can lawfully consecrate any place in his territory without his consent.[71]

C. *Vicar Capitular (Diocesan Administrator)*

The election, rights, privileges, duties and obligations of the vicar capitular are outlined in the Code.[72] In the United States and other places where no cathedral chapter exists, the diocesan consultors have the same right and duty as the cathedral chapter in electing a diocesan administrator who governs the diocese when the episcopal see is vacant.[73]

The vicar capitular, or in this country the administrator, who is endowed with the episcopal character may in virtue of his episcopal status validly consecrate churches in the diocese which he governs.[74] If the vicar capitular or diocesan administrator lacks the episcopal character, he cannot validly consecrate churches in his territory, unless he has obtained this faculty by means of an apostolic indult, for the Code does not attach that faculty to the office of a vicar capitular or diocesan administrator who lacks episcopal consecration.[75]

[68] Cf. canons 1147, § 1; 1155, § 1; 1157.

[69] Cf. canons 312-318.

[70] Canon 198, § 2.

[71] Cf. canons 1155, § 1; 1157.

[72] Canons 432-444.

[73] S. C. Consist., decr. *de nominandis administratoribus dioecesanis,* 22 febr. 1919—*AAS,* XI (1919), 75-76. See also S. C. Consist., decr. *Circa nominationem administratorum in dioecesibus vacantibus dominii Canadensis et Terrae Novae,* 8 maii 1919—*Ibid.,* p. 233.

[74] Canons 1147, § 1; 1155, § 1.

[75] Cf. canons 1147, § 1; 432-444.

The vicar capitular or diocesan administrator is a local ordinary, and no one may consecrate any place within his territory without his consent.[76] If the vicar capitular or diocesan administrator lacks the episcopal character, he may invite any bishop of the same rite to perform consecrations within the territory he governs.[77]

D. *Vicar General of a Residential Bishop*

The vicar general has by virtue of his office jurisdiction over the entire diocese in spiritual and temporal matters to the extent of the bishop's ordinary jurisdiction, except in those affairs which the bishop has reserved to himself, or which by law require a special mandate from the bishop.[78]

The consecration of a place is one of the affairs in which the vicar general lacks competence and therefore needs a special mandate from the bishop.[79] Even if the vicar general is a titular bishop, he may not perform the consecration nor may he give the necessary permission to another, unless he has a special mandate to that effect.[80] If the vicar general were a bishop and would consecrate a church without the mandate, the consecration would be valid,[81] but unlawful.[82]

Canon 1155, § 1 contemplates both a vicar general who has episcopal consecration, and a vicar general who lacks episcopal consecration. We will first consider a vicar general who has episcopal consecration and secondly, a vicar general who lacks episcopal consecration, and determine in each case their legal ability to validly and lawfully consecrate a place.

The act of consecrating a place is reserved exclusively to the local ordinary where the place is situated. A vicar general who has episcopal consecration in virtue of his episcopal consecration always consecrates a place validly, but for the lawfulness of the act, the vicar general who has episcopal consecration needs a special mandate

76 Cf. canons 198, § 2; 1157.
77 Canon 1155, § 2.
78 Canon 368, § 1.
79 Canon 1155, § 1.
80 Canon 1155, § 1.
81 Canon 1147, § 1.
82 Canons 1155, § 1; 1157.

from the local ordinary each time a place is to be consecrated by the vicar general who has episcopal consecration. This mandate is for the lawfulness of the act of consecrating a place.[83]

A vicar general who lacks the episcopal consecration is a local ordinary in virtue of canon 198, § 2, but the vicar general who lacks episcopal consecration cannot validly consecrate a place because canon 1147, § 1, invalidates an act of consecration performed by one who lacks episcopal consecration. The law does not grant the vicar general who lacks episcopal consecration the right to consecrate a place and the bishop is unable to delegate his own power of orders to a vicar general who lacks the episcopal consecration;[84] hence a vicar general who is not a bishop would need an apostolic indult to consecrate a place validly. The apostolic indult can be granted by the Roman Pontiff alone.[85]

E. *Vicar General of an Abbot or Prelate "Nullius"*

The abbot or prelate who possesses territorial jurisdiction must observe the rules of canons 366-371 in appointing a vicar general. These canons describe the appointment of a vicar general by a residential bishop, the requirements in the candidate for the office, and the duties, rights, and obligations of the vicar general.[86]

To avoid unnecessary repetition, it may simply be stated that what has been written about the vicar general of a residential bishop [87] in regard to the consecration of churches applies also in its entirety to the vicar general of an abbot or prelate who is a territorial ordinary.

F. *Pro-Vicar and Pro-Prefect Apostolic*

The Code in canons 309-311 describes the appointment, rights, duties, and obligations of the pro-vicar or pro-prefect apostolic who assumes the government of a vicariate or prefecture apostolic when the vicar or prefect is impeded in the exercise of his office.

[83] Cf. canons 1147, § 1; 1155, § 1; 1157.

[84] Cf. canon 210.

[85] Cf. canon 1147, § 1.

[86] Canon 323, § 3.

[87] Cf. Art. 4, D, of this chapter.

Those who in view of their devolved right rule a vicariate or prefecture must, according to canon 310, § 1, inform the Apostolic See of that fact as soon as possible. In the interim, they enjoy the faculties, both ordinary and delegated, which were enjoyed by the vicar or prefect, with the exception of those which were granted to the vicar or prefect in view of a special personal merit or qualification.[88]

The pro-vicar or pro-prefect has no power during the lifetime of the vicar or prefect, except such as is committed to him by his superior. When the pro-vicar or pro-prefect assumes the government of the vicarate or prefecture, and until the Holy See has made other provision, what has been written about the vicar or prefect apostolic in regard to the consecration of churches will apply also to the pro-vicar or pro-prefect.[89]

G. *Priests, Clerics in Major and Minor Orders, Laymen*

Before the Code it was argued whether a priest authorized by his local ordinary could validly consecrate a place. If a priest authorized by the bishop did consecrate a church, some believed that such an act could be tolerated.[90]

It has been noted that pre-Code authors explained that the bishop could not delegate his power of orders.[91] The Code in canon 1147, § 1, rules: "Consecrationes nemo qui charactere episcopali careat, validè peragere potest." This excludes a priest or anyone else who lacks episcopal consecration. The canon continues: ". . . nisi vel iure . . . id ei permittatur." The law however does not give to any simple priest the right to *consecrate* churches except to all cardinals, and to an abbot or prelate who possesses territorial jurisdiction. The canon finally states: ". . . nisi apostolico indulto id ei permittatur." This, then, can be the only source through which a priest can receive the power to validly consecrate a church.

88 Canon 310, § 2.

89 Cf. Art. 4, A, of this chapter.

90 *E. g.*, De Angelis, *Praelectiones Iuris Canonici*, lib. III, tit. 40, n. 3.

91 Cf. Art. 2, A (2) of this chapter.

Cappello [92] proposes several questions, namely, whether the Pope can delegate the power of consecrating a church not only to a priest, but also to clerics in major or minor orders, or even baptized Catholic laymen. The answer is in the affirmative, because as Cappello writes: "Tota res haec iuris mere ecclesiastici est, idcirco a voluntate R. Pontificis pendet ministrum designare, cui potestas sit, ecclesias aliasque res consecrandi.[93]

Article 5. The Consecration of a Church by a Suspended, Excommunicated, Heretical, Deposed or Degraded Bishop

The power of consecrating places is possessed by a bishop in virtue of his episcopal consecration.[94] The consecration of a church is an act of purely ecclesiastical authorization. The Church has annexed the right and the power of its performance to those who possess the episcopal character, in imitation of the power of Orders which by divine law is annexed to the episcopal character.[95] Therefore, just as a suspended, excommunicated, heretical, schismatical, deposed or degraded bishop, though all jurisdiction be taken away from him, is still able to confirm validly, and administer the sacrament of orders validly, so the same bishop can validly administer the sacramentals, *e. g.*, the consecration of a church,[96] provided that the essential rite prescribed by the Church be observed.[97]

Section II. The Minister of the Blessing of Churches

After his discussion concerning the minister for the valid and lawful consecration of a church, the writer will now consider the

[92] "De consecratione ecclesiarum,"—*Periodica,* XIX (1930), 139.

[93] *Loc. cit.*

[94] Cf. canon 1147, § 1.

[95] Cappello, "De consecratione ecclesiarum,"—*Periodica,* XIX (1930), 136; Maroto, "De ecclesiarum consecratione,"—*Apollinaris,* IV (1931), 245-250.

[96] Benedictus XIV, ep. *Iam inde,* 12 maii 1756, § 5—*Fontes,* II, n. 440; Coleman, *The Minister of Confirmation,* The Catholic University of America Canon Law Studies, n. 125 (Washington, D. C.: The Catholic University of America Press, 1941), p. 61; Gasparri, *De Ss. Eucharistia,* I, n. 156; Many, *De Locis Sacris,* n. 11.

[97] Canon 1148, § 2.

minister for the valid and lawful blessing of a church. The Code decrees that the right to bless a sacred place which belongs to the secular clergy, or to a non-exempt clerical religious or an exempt lay religious congregation, pertains to the ordinary of the territory where the place is situated; if the place belongs to an exempt clerical religious body, then the major religious superior has the right to bless it. Both the ordinary of the territory and the major superior of the religious community may delegate a priest for the blessing of places.[98]

Article 1. General Observations

The distinctions worthy of note between consecration and blessing are:

1. Consecrations performed by one lacking the episcopal character are invalid, unless permitted by law or by apostolic indult.[99]

Blessings may be given by any priest, with the exception of those which are reserved to the Roman Pontiff, to bishops, or to others. A reserved blessing, when given by a priest without the necessary permission, is unlawful but valid, unless in the reservation the Holy See has expressly stated otherwise. The consecration of a church by a bishop is always valid; the blessing of a church by a priest is always valid. The act may be unlawful if the bishop consecrates outside of his territory without the consent of the proper local ordinary; or if a priest blesses a church without proper delegation.[100]

2. The consecration of all places, even though they belong to regulars, is reserved to the local ordinary of the territory in which the place is situated.[101] The blessing of a place which belongs to the secular clergy, or to a non-exempt clerical religious, or an exempt lay religious congregation, is reserved to the local ordinary of the territory where the place is situated; if the place belongs to an exempt clerical religious body, then the major superior has the right to bless the place.[102]

[98] Canon 1156.

[99] Canon 1147, § 1.

[100] Canons 1147, §§ 2-3; 1157.

[101] Canons 1155, § 1; 1157.

[102] Canon 1156.

3. A bishop may give permission to another bishop of the same rite to *consecrate* places in his own proper territory, even such places as belong to regulars. The bishop may delegate a priest to *bless* a place that is under his jurisdiction.[103] The blessing of places which belong to an exempt clerical religious institute is reserved to the major superior, who may bless the place himself, or delegate a priest to perform the blessing.[104]

ARTICLE 2. THE MINISTER OF THE VALID AND LAWFUL BLESSING OF CHURCHES

The following are the valid and lawful ministers for the blessing of a church:

1. The local ordinary, for all churches in his territory, except those that belong to an exempt clerical religious body.[105]

2. The vicar general is not expressly excluded by law as in the case for consecration, and hence in virtue of his office the vicar general in regard to the *blessing* of places has the same right as the local ordinary, or the personal ordinary of an exempt group of religious.[106]

3. The major superior of regulars, for all places under his jurisdiction.[107] The term "major superior" is to be understood in the sense of canon 488, 8°.[108]

4. Any priest delegated by the local ordinary for places under his jurisdiction; or any priest delegated by the major superior of regulars for places under his jurisdiction.[109]

A priest who blesses a church without the necessary consent of the local ordinary, or of the major superior of regulars for churches under his jurisdiction, blesses the church validly but unlawfully, for a reserved blessing such as the blessing of churches, when performed by a priest without the necessary permission is unlawful but always

[103] Canons 1155, § 2; 1156.

[104] Canons 1156; 1157.

[105] Canon 1156.

[106] Canons 198; 1155, § 1; 1156. Cf. Vermeersch-Creusen, *Epitome*, II, n. 471.

[107] Canon 1156.

[108] Jone, *Gesetzbuch des kanonischen Rechtes*, II, 359.

[109] Canon 1156.

valid, unless in the reservation the Holy See has expressly stated that the blessing is invalid if it be performed without the necessary permission.[110] But the Code does not employ an invalidating clause in regard to the blessing of a place when it is performed by a priest without the necessary permission. Therefore, the blessing of a place by a priest without the necessary permission is always valid, but unlawful.[111] Furthermore, the Roman Ritual states: "Sacerdos novam ecclesiam seu oratorium publicum de licentia Ordinarii benedicturus. . . ." [112] This statement implies a clear indication that the blessing of a church is not exclusively reserved to the episcopal order, since the ordinary may delegate the blessing of a church to a priest. The right to bless places is reserved to the ordinary, but the rite of blessing is proper to those endowed with the power of the priesthood, and hence any validly ordained priest who blesses a church always acts validly, but unlawfully, if he lacks the necessary consent.[113]

The Roman Pontiff alone may delegate any cleric or even a layman to bless a church, since the conferring of a blessing is a matter merely of the proper ecclesiastical authorization.[114]

Schema

The following schema is proposed in order that the reader may more easily determine the minister and the power necessary to render the act of the blessing of churches, both valid and lawful.

[110] Canon 1147, § 3.

[111] Canons 1156; 1157.

[112] Tit. VIII, cap. 27, *Ritus benedicendi novam ecclesiam seu oratorium publicum.*

[113] Canon 1147, § 3. Cf. Coronata, *De Locis et Temporibus Sacris,* n. 5. See also De Angelis, *Praelectiones Iuris Canonici,* lib. III, tit. 40, n. 3; Many, *De Locis Sacris,* n. 17.

[114] Cf. what has been written in regard to consecration, Chapter VIII, Section I, Art. 4, G. pp. 97-98.

The act of blessing a church may be conferred

- I. As a reserved blessing both validly and lawfully
  - 1. by the local ordinary for all secular churches and also for all non-exempt religious churches within his territory
  - 2. by the major superior of an exempt religious institute for all the churches belonging to the institute
- II. As an act of the sacerdotal order
  - 1. validly, by all ordained priests
  - 2. lawfully, by all properly authorized priests
- III. As an act exercisable in virtue of the power of his office
  - 1. validly, by cardinals anywhere throughout the world
  - 2. lawfully, when the cardinals have the permission of the properly qualified ordinary
- IV. As an act flowing from delegated authorization both validly and lawfully
  - 1. by any cleric or layman who is authorized by the Supreme Pontiff
  - 2. by any priest who is authorized:
    - a. by the local ordinary in relation to the secular and non-exempt churches in his territory
    - b. by the religious ordinary in relation to the churches of his institute

CHAPTER IX

RECORD, PROOF, AND REPETITION OF CONSECRATION AND BLESSING

ARTICLE 1. NECESSITY FOR THE KEEPING OF THE RECORD

THE Code demands that a document be made attesting the fact of consecration or blessing. One copy shall be kept in the episcopal curia, and another in the archives of the respective church.

Canon 1158. De peracta consecratione vel benedictione redigatur documentum, cuius alterum exemplar in Curia episcopali, alterum in ecclesiae archivo servetur.

Blat adduces two reasons for the necessity of preserving a record after the consecration or blessing of a church.[1] The first is that many canons of the Code prohibit the performance of acts of divine worship except in a sacred place which has been dedicated by consecration or by blessing. The possession of a record attesting the fact that the place was consecrated or blessed will dispel any doubts that may arise in the future as to the fact of consecration or blessing of the place in question.

The second reason adduced by Blat is the Rule of Law: "Semel Deo dicatum, non est ad usus humanos ulterius transferendum." [2] A place that has been dedicated *(Deo dicatum)* to God by consecration or by blessing should not be used any more for profane uses, because of the reverence which is due to sacred things, which are effectively withdrawn from profane uses, and are thus set aside exclusively for a sacred use when they are dedicated to God.

To the reasons adduced by Blat another may be noted in the reference to the necessity of keeping a record of the consecration or blessing. The record will furnish proof not only of the fact of dedication, but also of the fact whether the church was consecrated or merely blessed. To avoid doubts and difficulties in the future, a properly authenticated document of the consecration or blessing is of

[1] *Commentarium,* III, n. 6.

[2] Reg. 51, R. J., in VI°.

the highest importance. Such a document is considered by law a public ecclesiastical document which contains full proof of the fact which it attests.[3]

In relation to the consecration and blessing of a church, such a record is extremely desirable and valuable, especially in view of the fact that there are certain obligations and privileges which arise in connection with a consecrated church, and which do not arise in connection with a church which has been dedicated solely by means of a blessing. The document will furnish legal proof of either the consecration or the blessing of a church should there be any doubt about the fact in the future. Hence it is important and necessary that a record of the consecration or blessing be properly preserved.

The Roman Pontifical [4] indicates by way of example what the minister of consecration should include on a small sheet of paper when he prepares the relics which are used for the consecration of an altar in conjunction with the consecration of a church, or for the consecration of an altar which takes place without the consecration of a church. The rubrics of the Roman Pontifical prescribe:

> "Sane sero ante diem Dedicationis, Pontifex parat Reliquias in Altari consecrando includendas, ponens eas in decenti et mundo vasculo, cum tribus granis thuris; ponit etiam in eo chartulam de pergamento, scriptam sub hac forma:
>
> *MCM, etc. . . . die N. mensis N. Ego N. Episcopus N.*[5] *consecravi Ecclesiam et altare hoc, in honorem Sancti N. et Reliquias Sanctorum Martyrum N. et N. in eo inclusi, et singulis Christi fidelibus hodie unum annum, et in die anniversario Consecrationis hujusmodi ipsam visitantibus* [in accordance with the law of canon 1166, § 3, or in agreement with the faculties granted by apostolic indult, the number of the days of indulgence granted is here to be expressed] *de vera Indulgentia, in forma Ecclesiae consueta concessi.*" [6]

[3] Canons 1813; 1816.

[4] Tit. *De ecclesiae dedicatione seu consecratione;* Tit. *De altaris consecratione, quae fit sine ecclesiae dedicatione.*

[5] If the minister of the consecration is not a bishop, but consecrates in virtue of the power inherent in his office or person, or by reason of an apostolic indult, this fact should be noted.

[6] Tit. *De ecclesiae dedicatione seu consecratione.*

The formula, proper allowance being made for the changed details, is the same when an altar is consecrated apart from the consecration of a church. When a church is blessed, the form as described above is not needed. But if a fixed altar is *consecrated* in conjunction with the blessing of a church, then the form demanded by the Roman Pontifical has to be drawn up. Relics are placed in a suitable container, which should be large enough to contain, besides the relics, three grains of incense, and a small piece of parchment, on which is written the form described in the Roman Pontifical, which attests the fact of consecration.[7]

The two formulas that are found in the Roman Pontifical relative to the consecration of a church, and the consecration of an altar which takes place without the consecration of a church, are not to be confused with the documents demanded by canon 1158 in attestation of the fact of consecration or blessing, of which documents one copy is to be kept in the episcopal curia, and another copy in the archives of the respective church.

Article 2. Place for the Keeping of the Record

The documents demanded by canon 1158 are to be made only after the consecration or blessing has taken place, and not before. This is suggested for practical reasons. Circumstances may unexpectedly impede the consecration or blessing on a particular day; the minister may not be able to complete the rite of consecration or blessing because of illness, etc. Hence, it is indicated that the documents be drawn up only after the consecration or blessing has been performed.

Two copies of the fact of consecration or blessing are demanded. One copy is to be kept in the episcopal curia;[8] the other copy is to be kept in the archives of the respective church.[9]

[7] Pontificale Romanum, Tit. *De altaris consecratione, quae fit sine ecclesiae dedicatione.*

[8] Cf. canon 375, § 1.

[9] Canon 1158; cf. canons 383-384; 470, § 4.

Beste,[10] Coronata,[11] De Meester [12] and Vermeersch-Creusen [13] write that, if a *blessed* church belongs to an exempt clerical institute, the document of the blessing need not be sent to the episcopal curia, but rather one copy is to be kept in the archives of the blessed church and the other copy could be kept in the archives of the exempt clerical institute, because the exempt clerical institute is not dependent on the local ordinary for any permission to *bless* their churches, as in the case of consecration.[14]

Ayrinhac [15] is indefinite in the matter, but implies that a copy of the document of both the consecration and the blessing "should perhaps be preserved in the archives of the order when the place thus consecrated or blessed belongs to exempt religious." [16] Ayrinhac's view cannot be held, for it lacks argument on any juridical basis. Ayrinhac does not exclude the bishop's archives as a place for a copy of the document of consecration or blessing of a place that belongs to exempt religious.[17]

Bondini [18] does not make any distinction. He simply states that the document attesting the fact of consecration or blessing of a church, even if the blessed church belongs to an exempt clerical order, is to be preserved in one copy in the archives of the particular church, and another copy in the episcopal curia. Bondini's view is in accord with canon 1158, which likewise does not make any distinctions or exceptions.

The Code distinguishes two types of archives that the bishop must provide in his diocese. Canon 375 describes the public or common archives, where all public documents pertaining to the spiritual and temporal affairs of the diocese are safely kept. Canon

[10] *Introductio in Codicem*, p. 555.

[11] *De Locis et Temporibus Sacris*, n. 6.

[12] *Juris Canonici et Juris Canonico-Civilis Compendium* (nova ed., 3 vols. in 4, Brugis, 1921-1928), n. 1116, footnote 4.

[13] *Epitome*, II, n. 472.

[14] Cf. canon 1156.

[15] *Administrative Legislation*, n. 4.

[16] Ayrinhac, *loc. cit.*

[17] Ayrinhac, *loc. cit.*

[18] *De Privilegio Exemptionis* (Romae: Desclée, 1919), n. 27.

379 describes the secret archives, in which documents relative to criminal cases, and other secret papers are kept. It is evident that canon 1158, which demands that a document of the consecration or blessing of a place be kept in the episcopal curia, has reference to the public archives described in canon 375.

It is true that when there is question of blessing a place that belongs to an exempt clerical order, the order does not need the consent of the local ordinary to bless the place, since according to canon 1156 the major superior may bless the place; but in regard to the document after the consecration or blessing has been performed, canon 1158 does not make any distinction, and simply decrees that one copy is to be kept in the episcopal curia, and the other in the archives of the respective church. Such a record in the episcopal curia is of vital importance for future use by those who have a right to use the record, as well as for the future students of history.

The law does not forbid the drawing up of more than two documents, but decrees that a copy is to be kept in the episcopal curia, and another copy in the archives of the respective church. This writer suggests that when a church which belongs to an exempt clerical order is blessed, three copies could be made in attestion of that fact: one copy to be sent to the episcopal curia, another copy to be kept in the archives of the blessed church, and a third copy to be kept in the archives of the religious institute.

Article 3. Proof of Consecration and Blessing

Whenever a doubt should arise as to the fact of the consecration or blessing of a church, the first proof to be adduced would naturally be furnished by the documents, as explained in the preceding article. If for some reason, however, these documents were lost or destroyed, then the law provides another method of proof.

The consecration or blessing of a church can be proved by one trustworthy witness, provided that no damage accrues to a third person in view of the acceptance of such a testimony.

Canon 1159, § 1. Consecratio vel benedictio alicuius loci, modo nemini damnum fiat, satis probatur eitam per unum testem omni exceptione maiorem.

The Code admits the evidence of one absolutely trustworthy witness, under the proviso that no one's rights are thereby injured. Excluding judicial proceedings in controversies about conflicting rights or claims, and likewise criminal cases, Canon Law accepts the reliable testimony of one witness in proof of a fact.[19] Thus proof of the reception of baptism [20] or of confirmation,[21] and also proof of the conferring of the consecration or blessing of a place [22] can be established canonically by the testimony of one absolutely trustworthy witness. When the Code admits the testimony of one witness in proof of a fact, it does so always on the condition that no damage accrue to a third party, or that his rights are not thereby called into question or compromised against his will.[23]

If no document or witnesses can be found, then other ways and means are admitted for establishing proof of the consecration or blessing of a church. Traces of the twelve crosses that were anointed at the time of the consecration would be sufficient proof for the consecration of the church. The constantly observed anniversary of the consecration would also suffice as a proof.[24]

Each case will vary and the circumstances will be different. Hence, if a doubt should arise about the consecration or blessing of a church, the doubt may be dispelled by the record of documents, by the testimony of witnesses, or by any other means which serve effectively in dispelling the doubt.

Article 4. Repetition of Consecration and Blessing

The Code forbids the repetition of the consecration or blessing of a place when legal proof is had that the consecration or blessing has taken place.

A church does not lose its consecration or blessing unless it is totally destroyed, or unless the greater part of the walls has collapsed,

[19] Coronata, *Institutiones Iuris Canonici,* III, n. 1323.

[20] Canon 779.

[21] Canon 800.

[22] Canon 1159, § 1.

[23] Cf. canon 1791, § 2.

[24] S. R. C., 27 nov. 1706—*Decr. Auth.*, n. 2174.

or unless the church has been reduced to secular purposes and uses by the authority of the local ordinary, according to the norm of canon 1187.[25] For a detailed study of the loss of consecration and blessing of a church, the reader is referred to commentators on the subject.[26]

When adequate proof is on hand regarding the conferring of the consecration or blessing of a church, any repetition of the consecration or blessing is forbidden for the same reason that rebaptism is not allowed, namely, because the ceremony imprints an indellible character.[27]

If a doubt about the conferring of the consecration or blessing cannot be dispelled, the Code calls for reconsecration or reblessing *"ad cautelam."* [28]

At times the fact of dedication by consecration or by blessing may be fully established by proof, but a doubt may exist about the validity of the consecration or blessing. If such a positive and reasonable doubt cannot be dispelled, then either the Holy See may be petitioned to grant a sanation, or else the law calls for the rite to be repeated as the canon decrees, *"peragatur ad cautelam."* [29]

Beste [30] states that when there is a reasonable and probable doubt about the fact of dedication, rededication is permitted. When the fact of dedication is known but there exists a doubt about the validity of the dedication, an option is had either to seek a sanation from the Holy See or repeat the rite of consecration conditionally.

Vermeersch-Creusen [31] in commenting on canon 1159, § 2, write:

[25] Cf. canon 1170.

[26] Ayrinhac, *Administrative Legislation,* n. 19; Beste, *Introductio in Codicem,* pp. 562-563; Coronata, *De Locis et Temporibus Sacris,* n. 26; Gulczynski, *The Desecration and Violation of Churches,* The Catholic University of America Canon Law Studies, n. 159 (Washington, D. C.: The Catholic University of America Press, 1942); Vermeersch-Creusen, *Epitome,* II, n. 486.

[27] C. 3, D. LXVIII; c. 16, 18, 20, D. I, *de cons.*; c. 111, D. IV, *de cons.*

[28] Canon 1159, § 2. "Si de ea legitime constet, nec consecratio nec benedictio iterari potest: in dubio autem, peragatur ad cautelam."

[29] Canon 1159, § 2.

[30] *Introductio in Codicem,* p. 555.

[31] *Epitome,* II, n. 473.

"Cum perpetuae sint per se tum consecratio, tum ipsa benedictio, prohibetur earum iteratio, si de alterutra legitime constet. In dubio autem *peragatur ad cautelam, i. e.,* iteratio permittitur. Observes aliud per se significari iteratione *condicionata,* aliud iteratione *ad cautelam* simpliciter concessa: haec est absoluta, sed propter iustam rationem permissa."

Augustine,[32] Ayrinhac [33] and Coronata [34] state that canon 1159, § 2, does not imply a conditional repetition of a doubtfully valid dedication, but, as the text of the canon states, points a procedure "*ad cautelam.*"

It is to be noted that the Church alone gives to a consecration or a blessing the dedicatory efficacy in consequence of which a place is constituted in a sacred character. Hence when a doubt exists about the dedication of a place in view of all possible lack of an earlier conferred consecration or blessing, the code calls for reconsecration or reblessing.[35]

The constant tradition of the Church has been to consecrate or bless a church whenever there was doubt about the fact of consecration or blessing. This is evident from testimony contained in a letter of Pope Gregory the Great (590-604) to Bishop Felix of Messina: [36]

"De dedicationum vero ecclesiarum dubitatione, . . . hoc vos rite tenere debetis, quod ab antecessoribus nostris traditum accepimus, id est, ut quoties tam de baptismo aliquorum vel confirmatione, quam de ecclesiarum consecratione dubitatio habetur, et nec scriptis nec testibus ratio certa habetur, utrum . . . ecclesiae consecratae sint, ut . . . ecclesiae canonicae dedicentur, ne talis dubitatio ruina fidelibus fiat, quoniam non monstratur iteratum, quod non certis indiciis ostenditur rite peractum."

Gratian (C. 1140) inserted the above text in his *Decretum.*[37] The practice of reconsecrating or reblessing churches because of their

[32] *A Commentary on Canon Law,* VI, 9.
[33] *Administrative Legislation,* n. 4.
[34] *De Locis et Temporibus Sacris,* n. 8.
[35] Cf. canon 1154, and canon 1159, § 2.
[36] *Epistolae,* lib. XIV, ep. XVII, *ad Felicem—MPL,* LXXVII, 1325.
[37] C. 16, D. I, *de cons.*

doubtful consecration or blessing as the Church's usual mode of procedure was evolved and sanctioned by Pope Benedict XIV,[38] and the teaching is now embodied in the Code.[39]

[38] Ep. *Iam inde,* 12 maii 1756, §§ 1-5—*Fontes,* n. 440.
[39] Canon 1159, § 2.

CHAPTER X

OBLIGATIONS COINCIDENT WITH AND SUBSEQUENT TO THE DEDICATION OF CHURCHES

Section I. **Coincident Obligations**

AFTER the minister of the consecration of a church has completed the ceremonies of consecration as prescribed in the Roman Pontifical, a rubric of the Roman Pontifical directs:

> "Tunc exit Pontifex Missam celebraturus. Si vero fatigatus nimis celebrare noluerit, facit Missam solemniter per aliquem sacerdotem celebrari." [1]

In regard to the above rubric of the Roman Pontifical Many wrote that except for the case of exhaustion the consecrating bishop would need an apostolic indult to allow a priest to offer Mass after the consecration ceremonies of a church were completed.[2] Holy Mass must be offered on the day of the consecration of a church. The Roman Pontifical prescribes that the bishop should celebrate Mass after the consecration ceremonies, but if the consecrating bishop feels fatigued after the ceremonies of consecration, for that reason he should provide that Mass is celebrated after the ceremonies of consecration.

The rubrics of the Missal prescribe the celebration of Mass on the day of the dedication of a church by blessing.

> "In ipsa die Dedicationis Ecclesiae, etsi ejus Officium ab Officio nobiliori impeditum fuerit, celebratur Missa de Dedicatione, ad modum votivae sollemnis pro re gravi." [3]

[1] Pontificale Romanum, tit. *De ecclesiae dedicatione seu consecratione.*

[2] Many, *De Locis Sacris,* n. 14, 3, b.

[3] *Additiones Et Variationes in Rubricis Missalis ad Normam Bullae "Divino Afflatu" Et Subsequentium S. R. C. Decretorum,* II, *De Missis Votivis,* 7. Hereafter cited, *Additiones Et Variationes in Rubricis Missalis.*

ARTICLE 1. CONSECRATED CHURCHES

A. *The Mass*

On the day that a church is consecrated the bishop who consecrated the church must at the conclusion of the ceremony offer Mass in the newly consecrated church. If the bishop is fatigued he must depute a priest to offer Mass. The Mass is celebrated as a Solemn Votive Mass and is the Mass *Terribilis est locus iste* as found in the *Commune Dedicationis Ecclesiae.* The oration is *Deus qui invisibiliter,* etc., the secret and post-communion prayers are those indicated by the rubrics in the Missal at the end of the Mass *Commune Dedicationis Ecclesia.* In this Mass of dedication is added under one conclusion with the principal oration the commemoration of the mystery or saint in whose honor the church is dedicated.[4]

The Missal directs:

> "Haec tamen Missa prohibetur in Duplicibus I classis Domini primariis universalis Ecclesiae, et in Dominica Palmarum; quibus diebus Commemoratio tantum Dedicationis et Titularis additur in Missa diei." [5]

When the rubrics prohibit the celebration of the Mass of the dedication of a church, the Mass of the day must be said and the commemoration of the dedication and the commemoration of the titular are added under one conclusion to the oration of the Mass of the day.[6]

Before the dedication of a church Mass can not be celebrated in the church.[7] If a priest who is attached to a church which is to

[4] ". . . et in ea, sub unica conclusione cum prima Oratione, additur Commemoratio Mysterii vel Sancti, in cujus honorem Ecclesia dedicatur."—*Additiones et Variationes in Rubricis Missalis,* II, 7.

[5] *Additiones et Variationes in Rubricis Missalis,* II, 7.

[6] For detailed rules about the celebration of Mass on the day of consecration and within the octave of the consecration of a church cf. De Herdt, *Sacra Liturgia,* III, n. 113; O'Connell, *The Celebration of Mass* (3 vols., Vol. I, *The General Rubrics of the Missal,* Bruce Publishing Co., Milwaukee, 1941), I, 81-83; Wapelhorst, *Compendium Sacrae Liturgiae,* n. 341; Wuest-Mullaney, *Matters Liturgical,* nn. 272-276.

[7] Cf. canon, 1165, § 1.

be consecrated must for any reason celebrate Mass in the church on the day of consecration, but before the consecration is performed, permission must be obtained from the bishop before the Mass is celebrated. The above applies when a church has not been dedicated either by consecration or by blessing. The bishop grants the permission to celebrate Mass in an undedicated church by virtue of canon 822, § 4. When a priest celebrates Mass on the day of the consecration of a church before the ceremonies of consecration are performed, the Mass will be according to the office of the day, and not the Mass *Commune Dedicationis Ecclesiae,* for the church is not as yet consecrated and the Mass *Commune Dedicationis Ecclesiae* presupposes that the church is consecrated. After the church is consecrated all Masses celebrated in the church on the day of consecration and during the octave must be of the *Commune Dedicationis Ecclesiae,* unless the rubrics prohibit this.[8]

B. *The Divine Office*

The laws of the liturgy and the decrees of the Holy See in regard to the recitation of the divine office *De Commune Dedicationis Ecclesiae* apply when a church has been dedicated by consecration, but not when the church is dedicated merely by blessing. The feast of the consecration of a church is to be celebrated by all the clergy attached to the church as a double of the first class with an octave, that is, as a feast of Our Lord.[9]

On the evening preceding the consecration of a church, when the consecrating minister has prepared the relics to be used in the consecration ceremonies of the altar, the clergy attached to the church that is to be consecrated recite Matins and Lauds from the *Commune plurimorum Martyrum.*[10] The lessons of the first nocturn are: "Fratres: Debitores sumus etc."; of the second nocturn:

[8] De Herdt, *Sacra Liturgia,* III, n. 113; O'Connell, *The Celebration of Mass,* I, 81-83; Schulte, *Consecranda,* p. 136; Wuest-Mullaney, *Matters Liturgical,* n. 273.

[9] S. R. C., 1 nov. 1911—*AAS,* III (1911), 646.

[10] S. R. C., 14 iun. 1845—*Decr. Auth.,* n. 2886; 18 aug. 1913—*Decr. Auth.,* n. 4306.

"Quotiescumque, fratres carissimi etc."; of the third nocturn: "Dominus ac Redemptor noster etc." The oration is the one which appears as n. 3 among the various orations listed in the *Commune:* "Deus qui nos annua sanctorum martyrum tuorum N. et N. solemnitate laetificas etc." But this oration becomes properly adapted for the occasion by the omission of the word *"annua"* and by the non-mention of any of the martyrs specifically.[11]

The office is a votive office like to that of a feast which is a primary double of the first class, and hence no commemorations are to be made. The recitation of Matins and Lauds from the *Commune plurimorum Martyrum* does not dispense one from the recitation of the current office of the day. The axiom, "officium pro officio valet," can not be applied.[12]

The office as described above is to be recited by all the clergy who are assigned to the church that is to be consecrated. The consecrating minister is not bound to recite the office. The feast is proper to the church that is to be consecrated, and hence only the clergy who are attached to the church that is to be consecrated are bound to recite the divine office on the evening preceding the consecration of their church.[13]

The office to be recited on the day of the consecration of a church is the one which is taken from the *Commune Dedicationis Ecclesiae.* It is distinct from the office recited on the vigil of the consecration. The office from the *Commune Dedicationis Ecclesiae* does not begin with the First Vespers, or Matins, but only with the Canonical hour which is to be recited after the consecration is completed, namely with Tierce,[14] for the office of the *Commune Dedicationis Ecclesiae* presupposes that the consecration of the church has taken place. First Vespers, Matins, Lauds and Prime are to be said according to the office of the day as prescribed in the *Ordo,* or Diocesan Calendar.[15] This office of the day is relinquished after the consecration of the

[11] S. R. C., 14 iun. 1845; 18 aug. 1913—*Loc. cit.*

[12] Beste, *Introductio in Codicem,* p. 560; Schulte, *Consecranda,* pp. 28-29.

[13] S. R. C., 7 maii 1746, ad 3—*Decr. Auth.,* n. 2390.

[14] S. R. C., 7 dec. 1844—*Decr. Auth.,* n. 2868.

[15] S. R. C., 29 iul. 1780, ad 5—*Decr. Auth.,* n. 2519.

church has taken place, and the consecrating minister is vesting for Mass. Tierce is then begun from the office of the *Commune Dedicationis Ecclesiae.*[16]

Article 2. Blessed Churches

A. *The Mass*

The Roman Ritual prescribes that Mass be celebrated after the ceremonies of the blessing of a church are completed.

> "His peractis, dicitur Missa de Mysterio vel Sancto, in cujus honorem ecclesia est benedicta." [17]

The bishop is not obliged to say this Mass. Another priest may celebrate the Mass after the bishop concludes the ceremonies of the blessing of a church. The Roman Ritual [18] and the Missal [19] demand that Mass be celebrated, but do not indicate that the minister who performed the blessing must also celebrate Mass.

The Mass to be celebrated at the conclusion of the ceremony of the blessing of a church is the Mass of the saint or mystery in whose honor the church is dedicated. This Mass enjoys the privileges of a *Missa votiva solemnis pro re gravi.*[20] If the blessing of a church is performed on a day when a *Missa votiva solemnis pro re gravi* is prohibited, then to the Mass of the day the commemoration of the titular shall be made under one conclusion according to the rubrics of the Missal.[21] For a full and complete description of the laws of the liturgy the reader may well consult the works of liturgists.[22]

[16] De Herdt, *Sacra Liturgia,* III, n. 113; Schulte, *Consecranda,* pp. 137-138; Wuest-Mullaney, *Matters Liturgical,* nn. 274, 737.

[17] *Rituale Romanum,* tit. VIII, cap. 27, n. 12, *Ritus benedicendi novam ecclesiam.*

[18] *Ritus benedicendi novam ecclesiam,* tit. VIII, cap. 27, n. 12.

[19] *Additiones et Variationes in Rubricis Missalis,* II, n. 9.

[20] *Additiones et Variationes in Rubricis Missalis,* II, n. 9.

[21] *Additiones et Variationes in Rubricis Missalis,* II, n. 9.

[22] O'Connell, *The Celebration of Mass,* I, 84; Schulte, *Benedicenda,* pp. 31-32; Wapelhorst, *Compendium Sacrae Liturgiae,* n. 341; Wuest-Mullaney, *Matters Liturgical,* nn. 280-281.

B. *The Divine Office*

The Code and the laws of liturgy do not indicate any special office on the occasion of the blessing of a church, nor on the anniversary of the blessing. Hence the clergy attached to a church that is to blessed are not bound to recite any special office on the day of the blessing of a church nor on the anniversary of the blessing.

Section II. **Subsequent Obligations**

The Code decrees that after a church has been consecrated the feast day of the consecration is to be celebrated annually, according to the norms of the laws of liturgy.

> **Canon 1167: Festum consecrationis ecclesiae quotannis celebretur ad normam legum liturgicarum.**

Canon 1167 prescribes the annual celebration of the dedication of a church only when the church is *consecrated,* and not when the church is merely *blessed.* There is no obligation to celebrate the anniversary of a church that was dedicated by blessing.

The feast of the consecration of a church and its anniversary are to be celebrated with Mass and the recitation of the divine office as a double of the first class with an octave, that is, as a feast of Our Lord.[23] The anniversary celebration of the consecration of a church is to be observed on the same date as that on which the church was consecrated, unless the bishop has at the time of consecration set another date for this anniversary function. The consecrating bishop has the right at the time of the consecration to choose the day for the annual celebration of the anniversary of the consecration of a church. The bishop can not select feasts of the First and Second class of the Church universal, a Sunday, or any feast of the First class in particular churches. At times the Holy See by special indult permits the celebration of the anniversary of all consecrated churches (except the cathedral church) in a diocese, a country, a religious order, or congregation on one and the same day.

[23] S. R. C., 4 febr. 1896, ad I—*Decr. Auth.*, n. 3881; S. R. C., 1 nov. 1911 —*AAS,* III (1911), 646.

All the clergy, secular and regular, who are favored by this indult, will celebrate this feast as of a double rite of the first class with an octave, provided that their own church is consecrated.[24]

It may be remarked that the Sacred Congregation of Rites [25] ruled that when by special indult the simultaneous celebration of the anniversary of the consecration of all the churches of a diocese on a special day was granted, all the clergy within the diocese, irrespective of the fact that their churches were not consecrated but merely blessed, or that some of the clergy were not attached to a church, were obliged to celebrate the anniversary of the dedication of all the churches of their dioccese as a double of the first class, with an octave.

The above ruling was changed by a later decree of the Sacred Congregation of Rites,[26] which decreed that the anniversary feast of the dedication of all the churches of a diocese on one and the same day must be understood in the sense that the anniversary is to be celebrated only in *consecrated* churches, and that each church celebrates its own consecration.[27]

The anniversary of the consecration of the cathedral church may not be celebrated together with the consecration anniversary of all the other churches of the diocese.[28]

Article 1. The Anniversary Mass and the Anniversary Divine Office

The rules given in Section I, Art. 1, of this chapter concerning the Mass and the divine office on the day of the consecration of a church and during the octave are also applicable to the anniversary celebration of the consecration of a church with one exception, namely,

[24] S. R. C., 19 sept. 1665, ad 3—*Decr. Auth.*, n. 1321; 6 sept. 1834, ad I—*Decr. Auth.*, n. 2719; 4 febr. 1896, ad I et V—*Decr. Auth.*, n. 3881; 28 oct. 1913, ad I, e, f—*Decr. Auth.*, n. 4308; 12 febr. 1914, ad I—*Decr. Auth.*, n. 4311.

[25] 9 iul. 1895, ad III—*Decr. Auth.*, n. 3863.

[26] S. R. C., 28 oct. 1913, ad I, f—*Decr. Auth.*, n. 4308; 12 febr. 1914, ad I—*Decr. Auth.*, n. 4311.

[27] S. R. C., 12 febr. 1914—*AAS*, VI (1914), 76; *Decr. Auth.*, n. 4311.

[28] S. R. C., 28 oct. 1913, ad I, e, f—*Decr. Auth.*, n. 4308; *AAS*, V (1913), 458.

the proper oration for the anniversary is said as found in the Missal and the Breviary for the *Commune Dedicationis Ecclesiae.* The anniversary of the consecration of a church is to be celebrated as a double of the first class, with an octave, by all the clergy attached to the consecrated church.[29] The clergy who are attached to a consecrated church and are therefore bound to observe the anniversary of the consecration are:

> ". . . omnes clerici qui habent in ea beneficium, vel ejus servitio, quocumque titulo canonico, sunt addicti, uno verbo, qui constituunt clerum hujus ecclesiae." [30]

With regard to cathedral churches the Sacred Congregation of Rites decreed that the anniversary of the consecration of the cathedral church is to be observed as a double of the first class, with an octave, by the secular clergy and also by those regulars who use the diocesan calendar. The regulars in the diocese who use a proper calendar must likewise keep the anniversary as a double of the first class, but without an octave.[31] The anniversary of the consecration of the cathedral church may not be celebrated together with the dedication of all the churches of the diocese, but must always be celebrated separately.[32] If the anniversary of the consecration of one's own church is to be celebrated on the same day as that of the cathedral church, the anniversary of the consecration of the cathedral church is transferred according to the rubrics. The rules for the occurrence and transfer of the feast of the dedication are are set forth in the general decrees of the Sacred Congregation of Rites.[33]

When a consecrated church has been execrated by any of the acts described in canon 1170, then the celebration of the anniversary of consecration becomes impossible. The pristine sanctity acquired

[29] S. R. C., 9 iul. 1895, ad III—*Decr. Auth.*, n. 3863 with the change as ruled by S. R. C., 28 oct. 1913, ad I, e, f—*Decr. Auth.*, n. 4308; *AAS*, V (1913), 458.

[30] Many, *De Locis Sacris,* n. 16.

[31] S. R. C., 28 oct. 1913—*Decr. Auth.*, n. 4308.

[32] S. R. C., 4 febr. 1896, ad V—*Decr. Auth.*, n. 3881.

[33] S. R. C., 4 febr. 1896—*Decr. Auth.*, n. 3881; S. R. C., 28 oct. 1913—*Decr. Auth.*, n. 4308.

by the church through its dedication is lost. Hence the anniversary celebration can not be observed.[34] A consecrated church that has been violated by any of the acts enumerated in canon 1172, § 1, retains its consecration. The performance of acts of divine worship are prohibited in a church that has been violated,[35] but the violation of a church does not deprive it of its consecration or blessing. Hence, after the reconciliation of a consecrated church which became violated the obligation of celebrating the anniversary of consecration is not suspended.[36]

Article 2. The Anniversary of the Titular Feast

One of the canonical requirements for the consecration or the blessing of a church is that the church must have a title. The titular feast of a consecrated or blessed church is to be celebrated annually according to the laws of the liturgy.

Canon 1168: Unaquaeque ecclesia consecrata vel benedicta suum habeat titulum; . . . Etiam festum tituli quotannis celebretur ad normas legum liturgicarum.

The church must be consecrated or blessed before the titular feast is celebrated. If a church were built and a title chosen and approved by the bishop, but the consecration or blessing were simply postponed, and the feast day commemorative of the mystery or of the personal titular of the church occurred, then the titular feast could not be celebrated, for the title is definitely constituted for the church only in the act of dedication. The title of a church is chosen in the blessing and laying of the corner-stone, but the definitive constitution of the title takes place only when the church is dedicated.[37]

The titular feast is to be celebrated with Mass and the recitation

[34] Coronata, *De Locis et Temporibus Sacris*, n. 23; Many, *De Locis Sacris*, n. 16.

[35] Canon 1173.

[36] S. R. C., 8 apr. 1713—*Decr. Auth.*, n. 2218.

[37] Pego, "De Titularibus et Patronis,"—*Ephemerides Liturgicae*, XXXIII (1919), 258-261.

of the divine office as a double of the first class with an octave.[38] The titular feast is to be celebrated annually on the day on which the feast of the titular or of the mystery occurs in the Church calendar, and by all the clergy attached to the particular church. This rule applies to all churches and public oratories which have been dedicated by consecration or blessing.[39] Semi-public oratories, episcopal chapels, the oratories of seminaries, hospital chapels, chapels of religious houses, oratories or chapels in army camps or at naval bases, and the main chapel of a cemetery are included, provided that they have been dedicated by blessing.[40]

A. *Clergy Obliged to Celebrate the Titular Feast*

The clergy strictly attached to a consecrated or blessed church are obliged to celebrate the titular feast in Holy Mass and in the recitation of the divine office. If perchance there are no clergy attached to the church, the titular feast should be observed at least in the celebration of Holy Mass.[41]

The following are considered strictly attached to a church, and hence are obliged to celebrate the titular feast:

1. All those who have a residential benefice in the church.[42]
2. The pastor and his assistants.[43] If two parish churches are

[38] S. R. C., 9 iul. 1895, ad II—*Decr. Auth.*, n. 3863: S. R. C., 8 iul. 1914—*Decr. Auth.*, n. 4324.

[39] S. R. C., 9 iul. 1895, ad II—*Decr. Auth.*, n. 3863.

[40] S. R. C., 5 iun. 1899—*Decr. Auth.*, n. 4025. Cf. *Rubricae in recitatione divini officii et in missarum celebratione servandae ad normam Constitutionis Apostolicae "Divino Afflatu,"* Tit. IX, *De Festis Dedicationis ac Tituli Ecclesiae et de Patronis*, nn. 1-2—*AAS*, III (1911), 646-647. The reader may well consult the works of the following liturgists: De Herdt, *Sacra Liturgia*, II, nn. 219-226; Pego, "De Titularibus et Patronis,"—*Ephemerides Liturgicae*, XXXIII (1919), 258-264, 329-334; Van Der Stappen, *Sacra Liturgia*, I, 380-410; Wapelhorst, *Compendium Sacrae Liturgiae*, nn. 339-340; Wuest-Mullaney, *Matters Liturgical*, nn. 726-736.

[41] S. R. C., 9 iul. 1895—*Decr. Auth.*, n. 3863; 5 iun. 1899, ad IV—*Decr. Auth.*, n. 4025.

[42] Pego, "De Titularibus et Patronis,"—*Ephemerides Liturgicae*, XXXIII (1919), 329; Gasparri, *De Ss. Eucharistia*, I, n. 144.

[43] S. R. C., 2 sept. 1871—*Decr. Auth.*, n. 3255; 11 aug. 1877, ad 1—*Decr. Auth.*, n. 3431; 18 aug. 1877, ad 3—*Decr. Auth.*, n. 3433.

held by one and the same pastor *(unio aeque-principalis)*, the pastor is obliged to observe the titular feast of both churches.[44]

3. Regulars who celebrate the feast of their own church. If there is a church attached to the monastery of regulars, but the regulars do not own the church, they are not allowed to celebrate the titular feast of that church. Likewise, if regulars live in a monastery to which no church is attached, they can not celebrate the titular feast of the church at which they attend for their religious services.[45]

4. The rector, the superiors, the seminary professors and the students (in major orders) who live in the seminary, for they are obliged to observe the titular feast of the seminary chapel.[46]

5. A bishop with reference to his cathedral church. If a bishop rules two dioceses *"aeque principaliter"* united, he is obliged to observe the titular feast of both cathedral churches if each has its own distinct title.[47]

6. A missionary assigned to several mission churches, but he is obliged to observe only the titular feast of the church with which his residence is connected.[48]

Chaplains of sisters are not bound to observe the titular feast of the chapel which they serve.[49]

B. *The Titular Feast of a Cathedral Church*

The titular feast of a cathedral church is to be celebrated as a double of the first class with an octave, and is to be celebrated by

[44] S. R. C., 27 apr. 1929—*AAS,* XXI (1929), 321; Beste, *Introductio in Codicem*, p. 561.

[45] S. R. C., 18 sept. 1877—*Decr. Auth.,* n. 3436; Pego, "De Titularibus et Patronis,"—*Ephemerides Liturgicae,* XXXIII (1919), 332-333.

[46] S. R. C., 27 febr. 1847, ad 3 et 5—*Decr. Auth.*, n. 2939; 18 sept. 1877—*Decr. Auth.*, n. 3436.

[47] S. R. C., 24 sept. 1842—*Decr. Auth.*, n. 2849.

[48] S. R. C., 25 aug. 1882—*Decr. Auth.*, n. 3554; 27 febr. 1883, ad II—*Decr. Auth.*, n. 3571.

[49] S. R. C., 12 nov. 1831—*Decr. Auth.*, n. 2682; Coronata, *De Locis et Temporibus Sacris*, n. 24, 7, b, *in fine*; Gasparri, *De Ss. Eucharistia,* I, n. 144; Pego, "De Titularibus et Patronis,"—*Ephemerides Liturgicae,* XXXIII (1919), 334.

all the clergy of the diocese, including the religious who follow the diocesan calendar. The religious who have their own calendar celebrate the titular feast of the cathedral church as a double of the first class without an octave.[50]

[50] Cf. *Rubricae in recitatione divine officii et in missarum celebratione servandae ad normam Constitutionis Apostolicae "Divino Afflatu,"* Tit. IX, *De Festis Dedicationis ac Tituli Ecclesiae et de Patronis,* nn. 1-2—*AAS,* III (1911), 646-647.

APPENDIX

INDULGENCES GRANTED AT THE CONSECRATION OF A CHURCH

Canon 1166, § 3: Cum consecratur ecclesia vel altare, Episcopus consecrator, licet iurisdictione in territorio careat, indulgentiam concedit unius anni ecclesiam vel altare visitantibus in ipsa consecrationis die; in die vero anniversaria quinquaginta dierum, si sit Episcopus; centum, si Archiepiscopus; biscentum, si S.R.E. Cardinalis.

THE Supreme Pontiff, Pope Pius XII on the occasion of his twenty-fifth episcopal consecration has augmented the faculties of bishops in the matter of granting indulgences. Abbots and prelates who are territorial ordinaries, vicars and prefects apostolic, and residential bishops may now grant 100 days' indulgence. Archbishops may grant 200 days' indulgence. Cardinals may grant 300 days' indulgence.[1]

In virtue of canon 1166, § 3, the consecrating bishop concedes an indulgence of one year to those who visit the church on the day of its consecration, even though the consecrating bishop has no jurisdiction over the territory. This is in derogation of canon 925, § 1,[2] which states that in order to gain an indulgence an individual must, in addition to meeting the other requisites, be a subject of the one who grants the indulgence. Even though the common law enjoins the granting of the indulgence, still, if the indulgence is to be made available for the faithful, it must be formally conceded by the consecrating bishop in connection with the ceremony of the consecration.[3]

[1] *AAS*, XXXIV (1942), 240; *The Jurist*, III (1943), 157-158.

[2] "Ut quis capax sit sibi lucrandi indulgentias, debet esse baptizatus, non excommunicatus, in statu gratiae saltem in fine operum praescriptorum, *subditus concedentis*."

[3] Vermeersch-Creusen, *Epitome*, II, n. 483.

The words "*episcopus consecrator*" of canon 1166, § 1, who concedes the indulgences on the occasion of the consecration and anniversary of the consecration of a church or altar no doubt have reference to a minister who consecrates a church or altar in virtue of ordinary power. This is imported from a response given by the Sacred Congregation of Rites, which declared:

> "... indulgentiae in consecratione altaris conceduntur ab episcopo qui altare consecrat, vel consecrare deberet, et tantum promulgantur ab ipso delegato." [4]

The apostolic indult must be consulted to determine the indulgences that are available on the occasion and anniversary of the consecration of a church when the consecrating minister performs the consecration in virtue of an apostolic indult.

[4] S. C. R., 26 oct. 1931 (private response)—*Archiv für katholiches Kirchenrecht*, CXIII (1933), 115. Cited also in Bouscaren, *Canon Law Digest*, I, p. 560.

CONCLUSIONS

1. After the Edict of Tolerance (313) it becomes evident from the testimony of definite documents that no church was used before it was dedicated, unless great necessity compelled the use of the building.

2. The dedicatory rite was not uniform in the Universal Church up to the time of the promulgation of the *Pontificale Romanum* by Pope Clement VIII in 1596. Every diocese had its particular usage.

3. The distinction of dedicating a church by means of a consecration or simply by means of a blessing was certainly introduced before the promulgation of the Decretals of Gregory IX in 1234.

4. The Code carefully distinguishes two forms for the dedication of a church: the one through consecration, the other by means of a blessing. The purely canonical effects attaching to the consecration or the blessing of a church are identical. The building becomes a sacred place, and divine services may then be conducted in the church.

5. A church in a combination building can be consecrated, provided that all the canonical requirements relative to the consecration of churches are observed.

6. A church in debt can be consecrated. There is no extant general legislation which demands that a church must be debt-free before it can be consecrated.

7. The clergy attached to a church and also the parishioners are not obliged to fast on the day preceding the consecration, if they have had no hand in requesting the consecration of their church.

8. The fast preceding the consecration of a church is regulated according to the common law regarding the ecclesiastical fast. If the vigil which precedes the day of the consecration of a church falls on a Sunday or a Feastday of obligation, then the fast is no longer of obligation on the Sunday or the Feastday, nor is it obligatory to anticipate the fast.

9. After the church has been dedicated either through consecration or by means of a blessing, the title of the church cannot be changed by the bishop without consulting the Holy See.

10. All cardinals, even though they lack the episcopal character, can consecrate churches validly everywhere; for the lawfulness of their act of consecration only the consent of the respective local ordinary is needed.

11. Abbots and prelates even though they lack the episcopal character can only consecrate churches validly in the territory over which they exercise jurisdiction. An abbot or prelate who has not the episcopal character cannot validly consecrate a church in another's territory even with permission of the ordinary of that territory. To validly consecrate a church outside his territory an abbot or prelate with territorial jurisdiction who lacks the episcopal character needs an apostolic indult.

12. A priest can bless churches validly even without the permission of the local ordinary. The act without permission is unlawful.

13. Major superiors in exempt communities need no permission to bless their church.

14. The Supreme Pontiff can delegate priests to consecrate and other clerics and laymen to bless.

15. Vicars and prefects apostolic can not consecrate ex officio.

16. Two documents must be drawn up in attestation of the fact of the consecration or the blessing of a church. One copy is to be kept in the episcopal curia, and the other copy in the archives of the respective church, even when the consecrated or blessed church belongs to an exempt clerical institute. The law does not forbid the drawing up of more than two documents.

BIBLIOGRAPHY

Sources

Acta Apostolicae Sedis, Commentarium Officiale, Romae, 1909.

Acta et Decreta Sacrorum Conciliorum Recentiorum, Collectio Lacensis, 7 vols., Friburgi Brisgoviae, 1870-1892.

Acta Sanctae Sedis, 41 vols., Romae, 1865-1908.

Bouscaren, T. Lincoln, *The Canon Law Digest,* 2 vols., and Supplement—1941, Milwaukee: Bruce, 1934-1941.

Breviarium Romanum ex Decreto SS. Concilii Tridentini Restitutum S. Pii V Pontificis Maximi Jussu Editum Aliorumque Pont. Cura Recognitum Pii Papae X Auctoritate Reformatum, Ratisbonae: Sumptibus et Typis Friderici Pustet, 1936.

Bullarum Diplomatum et Privilegiorum Romanorum Pontificum Taurinensis Editio, 25 vols., Augustae Taurinorum, 1857-1872.

Bullarium SSmi. Domini Nostri Benedicti Papae XIV, 4. ed., 4 vols., Venetiis, 1778.

Codex Iuris Canonici Pii X Pontificis Maximi iussu digestus, Benedicti Papae XV auctoritate promulgatus, Romae: Typis Polyglottis Vaticanis, 1917. Reimpressio, 1933.

Codicis Iuris Canonici Fontes cura Emi. Petri Card. Gasparri editi, 9 vols. Romae (postea Civitate Vaticana): Typis Polyglottis Vaticanis, 1923-1939. (Vols. VII-IX ed. cura et studio Emi. Iustiniani Card. Serédi.)

Corpus Iuris Canonici, ed. Lipsiensis 2. post Aemilii Ludovici Richteri curas . . . instruxit Aemilius Friedberg, Lipsiae: Ex Officina Bernhardi Tauchnitz, 1879-1881. Edito anastatice repetita, Lipsiae: Tauchnitz, 1928.

Corpus Iuris Civilis, 3 vols., Berolini, 1928-1929. *Institutiones,* quas recognovit P. Krueger; *Digesta,* quae recognovit et retractavit P. Krueger; *Codex Iustinianus,* quem recognovit et retractavit P. Krueger; *Novellae,* quas recognovit R. Schoell, et absolvit G. Kroll.

Decreta Authentica Congregationis Sacrorum Rituum ex Actis eiusdem collecta eiusque auctoritate promulgata sub auspiciis SS. D. N. Leonis Papae XIII, 6 vols., Romae, 1898-1927.

Decretales D. Gregorii IX una cum Glossis Restitutae, Romae, 1582.

Decretum Gratiani Emendatum et notationibus illustratum una cum Glossis, Gregorii XIII, Pont. Max. iussu editum, 2 vols., Romae, 1852.

Gardellini, Aloisius, *Decreta Authentica Congregationis Sacrorum Rituum ex actis eiusdem collecta,* 3. ed., 4 vols., cum appendicibus usque ad annum 1887, Romae, 1856-1887.

Hardouin, Jean, *Acta Conciliorum et Epistolae Decretales ac Constitutiones Summorum Pontificum,* 12 vols., Paris, 1714-1715.

Jaffé, Philippus, *Regesta Pontificum Romanorum ab condita Ecclesia ad annum post Christum natum MCXCVIII,* ed. 2. correctam et auctam auspiciis Gulielmi Wattenbach curaverunt S. Loewenfeld, F. Kaltenbrunner, P. Ewald, 2 vols. in 1, Lipsiae: 1885-1888.

Liber Sextus Decretalium D. Bonifacii Papae VIII suae integritati una cum Clementinis et Extravagantibus earumque Glossis restitutis, Romae: 1582.

Mansi, Ioannes Dominicus, *Sacrorum Conciliorum Nova et Amplissima Collectio,* 53 vols. in 59, Paris-Arnhem-Leipzig: 1901-1927.

Missale Romanum ex Decreto Sacrosancti Concilii Tridentini Restitutum, S. Pii V Pontificio Maximi iussu editum, Aliorum Pontificum cura Recognitum, a Pio X Reformatum et SSmi. D. N. Benedicti XV auctoritate vulgatum, Ratisbonae: Sumptibus et Typis Friderici Pustet, 1925.

Monumenta Germaniae Historica, Legum Sectio III, *Concilia* Tomus I, *Concilia Aevi Merovingici* (Recensuit Friedericus Maassen), Hannoverae, 1893.

Pontificale Romanum Summorum Pontificum iussu editum a Benedicto XIV et Leone XIII Pontificibus Maximis recognitum et castigatum, Ratisbonae, 1891.

Rituale Romanum Pauli V Pontificis Maximi Jussu Editum Aliorumque Pontificum Cura Recognitum Atque Auctoritate SSmi. D. N. Pii Papae XI ad normam Codicis Juris Canonici accommodatum, Ratisbonae: Sumptibus et Typis Friderici Pustet, 1925.

Schroeder, H. J., *Canons and Decrees of the Council of Trent: Original Text with English Translation,* St. Louis: B. Herder Book Co., 1941.

———, *Disciplinary Decrees of the General Councils,* St. Louis: B. Herder Book Co., 1937.

Theodosiani Libri XVI cum Constitutionibus Sirmondianis, Edidit, adsumpto apparatu P. Kruegeri, Th. Mommsen, Berolini: apud Weidmannos, 1905.

Reference Works

Augustine, Charles, *A Commentary on the New Code of Canon Law,* 8 vols., St. Louis: Herder, Vol, VI, *Administrative Law,* 3. ed., 1931.

———, *Liturgical Law,* St. Louis: Herder, 1931.

Ayrinhac, H. A., *Administrative Legislation in the New Code of Canon Law,* New York: Longmans, Green & Co., 1930.

———, *Constitution of the Church in the New Code of Canon Law,* London-New York- Toronto: Longmans, Green & Co., 1930.

Benedictus XIV, *De Sacrosancto Missae Sacrificio,* Prati, 1843.

———, *De Synodo Dioecesana,* 2 vols., Ferrariae, 1775.

Beste, Udalricus, *Introductio in Codicem,* Collegeville, Minnesota: St. John's Abbey Press, 1938.

Bingham, Joseph, *The Antiquities of the Christian Church*, 2 vols., London, 1856.

Blat, Albertus, *Commentarium Codicis*, 6 vols., Romae, 1921-1924, Vol. III, *De Rebus*, Partes II-VI, 1923.

Bliley, Nicholas Martin, *Altars According to the Code of Canon Law*, The Catholic University of America Canon Law Studies, n. 38, Washington, D. C.: The Catholic University of America Press, 1927.

Bona, Ioannes Card., *Rerum Liturgicarum Libri Duo*, Romae, 1671.

Bondini, A., *De Privilegio Exemptionis*, Romae, 1919.

Bouix, D., *Institutiones Iuris Canonici, Tractatus de Jure Liturgico*, Parisiis, 1860.

Braun, Joseph, *Der christliche Altar in seiner geschichtlichen Entwicklung*, 2 vols., Munich, 1924.

Buonocore, Guiseppe, *Il "Titulus Canonicus,"* 2 vols., Napoli, 1933.

Callewaert, C., *Liturgicae Institutiones: Tractatus primus de S. Liturgia universim*, editio tertia recognita et aucta, Brugis: Beyaert, 1933.

Catalanus, Josephus, *Pontificale Romanum*, ed. nova, 3 vols., Parisiis, 1850-1852.

———, *Rituale Romanum Benedicti Papae XIV Jussu Editum et Auctum, Perpetuis Commentariis Exornatum ac in duos Tomos divisum*, Patavii, 1760.

Cavalieri, Joannes, *Opera Omnia Liturgica, Seu Commentaria*, Quinque Tomis Comprehensa, Venetiis, 1758.

Cicognani, Amleto Giovanni, *Canon Law*, 2. ed., authorized English version by J. O'Hara and F. Brennan, Philadelphia: Dolphin Press, 1935.

Coleman, John Jerome, *The Minister of Confirmation*, The Catholic University of America Canon Law Studies, n. 125, Washington, D. C.: The Catholic University of America Press, 1941.

Collins, Harold E., *The Church Edifice and Its Appointments*, 2. ed., Philadelphia, The Dolphin Press, 1940.

Coronata, Mathaeus Conte a., *De Locis et Temporibus Sacris*, Taurini: Marietti, 1922.

———, *Compendium Iuris Canonici*, 2 vols., Taurini: Marietti, 1937-1938.

De Angelis, Philippus, *Praelectiones Iuris Canonici, ad Methodum Decretalium Gregorii IX Exactae*, 4 vols., in 6, Romae: 1877-1887.

De Bonis, Iosephus, *De Oratoriis Publicis*, Mediolani, 1761.

De Herdt, P. J. B., *Sacrae Liturgiae Praxis*, 3 vols., Louvanii, 1889.

De Puniet, Pierre, *The Roman Pontifical*, London, New York, Toronto: Longmans, Green & Co., 1932.

De Meester, A., *Juris Canonici et Juris Canonico-Civilis Compendium*, nova editio, 3 vols. in 4, Brugis, 1921-1928.

De Rossi, G. B., *Roma Sotterranea Cristiana,* 3 vols., Romae, 1864-1877.

De Rozière, Eugene, *Liber Diurnus ou Recueil des Formules usitées par la Chancellerie Pontificale du Ve au XIe siècle,* Paris, 1869.

Devoti, Ioannes, *Institutionum Canonicarum Libri IV,* 3 vols., Romae, 1860.

Dooley, Eugene A., *Church Law on Sacred Relics,* The Catholic University of America Canon Law Studies, n. 70, Washington, D. C.: The Catholic University of America Press, 1927.

Duchesne, Louis, *Christian Worship,* translated by M. J. McClure, 5. ed., London: Society for the Promotion of Christian Knowledge, 1931.

——, *Le Liber Pontificalis,* 2 vols., Paris, 1886-1892.

Durantus, Ioannes Stephanus, *De Ritibus Ecclesiae Catholicae Libri Tres,* Lugduni, 1608.

Feldhaus, Aloysius H., *Oratories,* The Catholic University of America Canon Law Studies, n. 42, Washington, D. C.: The Catholic University of America Press, 1927.

Feltoe, C., *Sacramentarium Leonianum,* Cambridge, 1896.

Ferraris, F. Lucius, *Prompta Bibliotheca, Canonica, Juridica, Moralis, Theologica, necnon Ascetica, Polemica, Rubricistica, Historica,* ed. Migne, 8 vols., Parisiis, 1860-1863.

Ferreres, Ioannes, *Institutiones Canonicae,* Barcinone, 1918.

Fortescue, A.-O'Connell, J. B., *The Ceremonies of the Roman Rite Described,* 6. ed., London: Burns, Oates & Washbourne, Ltd., 1937.

Gasparri, Petrus, *De SS. Eucharistia,* 2 vols., Parisiis et Lugduni, 1897.

——, *De Sacra Ordinatione,* 2 vols., Parisiis, 1893-1894.

Gatticus, Ioannes Baptista, *De Oratoriis Domesticis,* Romae, 1770.

Gonzalez-Tellez, Manuel, *Commentaria Perpetua in singulos textus Quinque Libros Decretalium Gregorii IX,* 5 vols., in 4, Venetiis, 1699.

Grabowski, Ignacy, *Prawo Kanoniczne Wedlug Nowego Kodeksu,* Bibljoteka Religijna, Lwow, Poland, 1927.

Guiniven, John Joseph, *The Precept of Hearing Mass,* The Catholic University of America Canon Law Studies, n. 158, Washington, D. C.: The Catholic University of America Press, 1942.

Gulczynski, J., *The Desecration and Violation of Churches,* The Catholic University of America Canon Law Studies, n. 159, Washington, D. C.: The Catholic University of America Press, 1942.

Heston, Edward Louis, *The Alienation of Church Property in the United States,* The Catholic University of America Canon Law Studies, n. 132, Washington, D. C.: The Catholic University of America Press, 1941.

Hinschius, Paul, *Decretales Pseudo-Isidorianae,* Leipzig, 1863.

——, *Das Kirchenrecht der Katholiken und Protestanten in Deutschland,* 6 vols., Berlin, 1869-1897.

Jone, Heribert, *Gesetzbuch des kanonischen Rechtes,* 3 vols., Paderborn: Ferdinand Schöningh, 1939-1941.

Laemmer, Hugo, *Eusebii Pamphili Historia Ecclesiastica,* Scaphusiae, 1862.

Loeb Classical Library, The, edited by E. Capps, T. E. Page, W. H. D. Rouse, Eusebius, *The Ecclesiastical History* (with an English translation by Kirsopp Lake), in 2 vols., New York: G. P. Putnam's Sons, 1926.

Mabillon, John, *Museum Italicum,* 2 vols., Paris, 1687-1689.

McDonough, Thomas Joseph, *Apostolic Administrators,* The Catholic University of America Canon Law Studies, n. 139, Washington, D. C.: The Catholic University of America Press, 1941.

Many, S., *Praelectiones de Locis Sacris,* Parisiis, 1904.

Martène, Edmund, *De Antiquis Ecclesiae Ritibus,* 4 vols., Ratomagi, 1700-1706.

Migne, Jacques Paul, *Patrologiae Cursus Completus, Series Latina,* 221 vols., Parisiis, 1844-1864.

———, *Patrologiae Cursus Completus, Series Graeca,* 161 vols., Parisiis, 1856-1866.

Muratori, Ludvicus A., *Liturgia Romana Vetus,* 2 vols., Venetiis, 1748.

O'Connell, J., *The Celebration of Mass,* 3 vols., Vol. 1, *The General Rubrics of the Missal,* Milwaukee: Bruce Publishing Co., 1941.

Ojetti, Benedictus, *Synopsis Rerum Moralium et Iuris Pontificii,* Romae, 1899.

Pirhing, Ernricus, *Jus Canonicum Nova Methodo Explicatum,* 5 vols. in 4, Dilingae, 1674-1678.

Reiffenstuel, Anacletus, *Ius Canonicum Universum,* 5 vols. in 7, Parisiis, 1864-1882.

Santi, Franciscus, *Praelectiones Juris Canonici,* 2 vols., Ratisbonae, Neo-Eboraci, Cincinnati, 1886.

Schmalzgrueber, Franciscus, *Ius Ecclesiasticum Universum,* 5 vols. in 12, Romae, 1843-1845.

Schulte, A. J., *Benedicenda,* New York, Cincinnati, Chicago, 1907.

———, *Consecranda,* New York, Cincinnati, Chicago, 1907.

Schuster, Ildefonso, *The Sacramentary (Liber Sacramentorum),* translated from the Italian by Arthur Levelis-Marke, 5 vols., London: Burns, Oates & Washbourne, Ltd., 1924.

Sextus, Pompeius Festus (fl. c. 300), *De Verborum Significatione,* Romae, 1826.

Smith, William-Cheetham, Samuel, *A Dictionary of Christian Antiquities,* 2 vols., Hartford, 1880.

Stenger, Joseph Bernard, *The Mortgaging of Church Property,* The Catholic University of America Canon Law Studies, n. 169, Washington, D. C.: The Catholic University of America Press, 1942.

Suarez, Franciscus, *Opera Omnia,* editio nova, 30 vols., Vol. XXVII, *De Sacramento Eucharistiae,* Parisiis, 1866.

Thalhofer, Valentine, *Handbuch der katolischen Liturgik,* 2 vols., Freiburg im Breisgau, 1883-1890.

Thomassinus, Ludovicus, *Vetus et Nova Ecclesiae Disciplina circa Beneficia et Beneficiarios,* 10 vols., Parisiis, 1786-1787.

Toso, Alberto, *Commentaria Minora ad Codicem Iuris Canonici,* Città de Castello, 1921.

Van der Stappen, J. F., *Sacra Liturgia,* 5 vols., Mechliniae, 1900-1904.

Van Hove, A., *Commentarium Lovaniense in Codicem Iuris Canonici,* Vol. I, Tom. I, *Prolegomena,* Mechliniae-Romae: H. Dessain, 1928.

Varro, Marcus Terentius, *De Lingua Latina,* Romae, 1821.

Vermeersch, A.-Creusen, J., *Epitome Iuris Canonici,* 3 vols., Vol. II, 6. ed., Mechliniae-Romae: H. Dessain, 1940.

Wapelhorst, Innocentius, *Compendium Sacrae Liturgiae,* 11 ed., New York: Benziger Brothers, 1931.

Wernz, Franciscus X., *Ius Decretalium,* 6 vols., Romae et Prati, 1898-1905, Tomus III, *Ius Administrationis,* 1901.

Wernz, Franciscus X.-Vidal, Petrus, *Ius Canonicum,* 7 vols. in 8, Romae, Apud Aedes Universitatis Gregorianae, 1923-1938, Tomus IV (*De Rebus*), Vol. 1, 1934.

Wilson, H., *The Gelasian Sacramentary,* Oxford, 1894.

———, *The Gregorian Sacramentary,* London, 1915.

Woywod, S., *A Practical Commentary on the Code of Canon Law,* 5. revised edition, 2 vols., New York: Wagner, 1939.

Wuest, Joseph-Mullaney, Thomas W., *Matters Liturgical,* 4. ed., New York: Frederick Pustet, 1934.

Zaccaria, F., *Bibliotheca Ritualis,* Romae, 1776-1781.

PERIODICALS

Apollinaris, Romae, 1928—

Australasian Catholic Record, The, Manly, 1923—

Catholic Historical Review, The, Washington, 1915—

Clergy Review, The, London, 1931—

Ephemerides Liturgicae, Commentarium cura et studio Presbyterorum Congregationis Missionis Nonnullis Doctis Variis Adlaborantibus Alternis Mensibus Editum, Roma: Via Pompeo Magno, 21, 1887—

Irish Ecclesiastical Record, The, Dublin, 1864—

Jurist, The, Washington, D. C., 1941—

Periodica de Re Canonica et Morali utili praesertim Religiosis et Missionariis, Brugis, 1905—; ab anno 1927: *Periodica de Re Morali, Canonica, Liturgica.*

Articles

Barin, Aloisius, "Commentarium ad Canones C. I. C. sacram Liturgiam spectantes"—*Ephemerides Liturgicae,* XXXVI (1922), 16-17; XXXVII (1923), 58.

Bastnagel, C. V., "Cases and Studies"—*The Jurist,* II (1942), 155-158.

Cappello, Felix, "De Consecratione Ecclesiarum"—*Periodica,* XIX (1930), 135.

———, "Annotationes, III"—*Periodica,* XVIII (1929), 253.

Mahoney, E. J., "Parish Hall in Church Basement"—*The Clergy Review,* XXII (1942), 131-132.

Maroto, Philippus, "De Ecclesiae Consecratione"—*Apollinaris,* IV (1931), 243-250.

———, "De Ieiunio in Consecratione Ecclesiae"—*Apollinaris,* III (1930), 238.

Nevin, J., "A Mortgage on the Parochial Church"—*The Australasian Catholic Record,* X (1933), 348-351.

———, "Heavy Debt on Church—May Altar Be Consecrated?"—*The Australasian Catholic Record,* XV (1938), 259-260.

Pego, Augustinus, "De Titularibus et Patronis"—*Ephemerides Liturgicae,* XXXIII (1919), 256-264; 329-334.

Ziegler, A. K., "Pope Gelasius I and His Teaching on the Relation of Church and State"—*The Catholic Historical Review,* XXVII (1942), 412-437.

ABBREVIATIONS

AAS—*Acta Apostolicae Sedis.*
ACR—*Australasian Catholic Record.*
ASS—*Acta Sanctae Sedis.*
Bull. Rom.—*Bullarum Diplomatum . . . Romanorum Pontificum Taurinensis Editio.*
C.—Codex (Iustinianus).
C. Th.—Codex Theodosianus.
D.—Digestum (Iustinianum).
Decr. Auth.—*Decreta Authentica Congregationis Sacrorum Rituum . . . sub auspiciis SS. D. N. Leonis Papae XIII.*
Ferraris—*Prompta Bibliotheca,* etc.
Fontes—*Codicis Iuris Canonici Fontes cura . . . Gasparri editi.*
Hardouin—*Acta Conciliorum,* etc.
IER—*Irish Ecclesiastical Record.*
Jaffé—*Regesta Pontificum Romanorum,* etc.
Mansi—*Sacrorum Conciliorum Nova et Amplissima Collectio.*
MGH—*Monumenta Germaniae Historica.*
MPG—Migne, *Patrologia, Series Graeca.*
MPL—Migne, *Patrologia, Series Latina.*
N—Novellae (Iustinianae).
PCI—*Pontificia Commissio ad Codicis Canones Authentice Interpretandos.*
Periodica—*Periodica de Re Morali, Canonica, Liturgica,* etc.
S. C. C.—Sacra Congregatio Concilii.
S. C. Sacr.—Sacra Congregatio de disciplina Sacramentorum.
S. R. C.—Sacrorum Rituum Congregatio.

ALPHABETICAL INDEX

BIOGRAPHICAL NOTE

THADDEUS STANISLAUS ZIOLKOWSKI was born September 15, 1912, in Hazleton, Pennsylvania. He received his elementary education in the Catholic schools, and his secondary education in public schools of that city. In the fall of 1930, he matriculated at St. Mary's College, Orchard Lake, Michigan, and received the Bachelor of Arts degree in 1934. He completed his theological studies at St. Francis' Seminary, Loretto, Pennsylvania, and was ordained to the priesthood for the Diocese of St. Cloud, Minnesota, on May 26, 1938. After two years of parochial work in the Diocese of St. Cloud, Minnesota, he enrolled, in September, 1940, in the School of Canon Law at The Catholic University of America, where he received the degree of Baccalaureate in Canon Law in June, 1941, and the degree of Licentiate in Canon Law in May, 1942.

CANON LAW STUDIES *

1. FRERIKS, REV. CELESTINE A., C.PP.S., J.C.D., Religious Congregations in Their External Relations, 121 pp., 1916.
2. GALLIHER, REV. DANIEL M., O.P., J.C.D., Canonical Elections, 117 pp., 1917.
3. BORKOWSKI, REV. AURELIUS L., O.F.M., J.C.D., De Confraternitatibus Ecclesiasticis, 136 pp., 1918.
4. CASTILLO, REV. CAYO, J.C.D., Disertacion Historico-Canonica sobre la Potestad del Cabildo en Sede Vacante o Impedida del Vicario Capitular, 99 pp., 1919 (1918).
5. KUBELBECK, REV. WILLIAM J., S.T.B., J.C.D., The Sacred Penitentiaria and Its Relation to Faculties of Ordinaries and Priests, 129 pp., 1918.
6. PETROVITS, REV. JOSEPH, J.C., S.T.D., J.C.D., The New Church Law on Matrimony, X-461 pp., 1919.
7. HICKEY, REV. JOHN J., S.T.B., J.C.D., Irregularities and Simple Impediments in the New Code of Canon Law, 100 pp., 1920.
8. KLEKOTKA, REV. PETER J., S.T.B., J.C.D., Diocesan Consultors, 179 pp., 1920.
9. WANENMACHER, REV. FRANCIS, J.C.D., The Evidence in Ecclesiastical Procedure Affecting the Marriage Bond, 1920 (Printed 1935).
10. GOLDEN, REV. HENRY FRANCIS, J.C.D., Parochial Benefices in the New Code, IV-119 pp., 1921 (Printed 1925).
11. KOUDELKA, REV. CHARLES J., J.C.D., Pastors, Their Rights and Duties According to the New Code of Canon Law, 211 pp., 1921.
12. MELO, REV. ANTONIUS, O.F.M., J.C.D., De Exemptione Regularium, X-188 pp., 1921.
13. SCHAAF, REV. VALENTINE THEODORE, O.F.M., S.T.B., J.C.D., The Cloister, X-180 pp., 1921.
14. BURKE, REV. THOMAS JOSEPH, S.T.D., J.C.D., Competence in Ecclesiastical Tribunals, IV-117 pp., 1922.
15. LEECH, REV. GEORGE LEO, J.C.D., A Comparative Study of the Constitution "Apostolicae Sedis" and the "Codex Juris Canonici," 179 pp., 1922.
16. MOTRY, REV. HUBERT LOUIS, S.T.D., J.C.D., Diocesan Faculties According to the Code of Canon Law, II-167 pp., 1922.
17. MURPHY, REV. GEORGE LAWRENCE, J.C.D., Delinquencies and Penalties in the Administration and the Reception of the Sacraments, IV-121 pp., 1923.
18. O'REILLY, REV. JOHN ANTHONY, S.T.B., J.C.D., Ecclesiastical Sepulture in the New Code of Canon Law, II-129 pp., 1923.

* Below n. 100 only the following numbers are still available: Nn. 3, 4, 9, 25, 34, 57 and 75. Beginning with n. 100 only the following are unavailable: Nn. 100, 101, 102, 104, 105, 107, 108, 109, 111 and 113.

19. Michalicka, Rev. Wenceslas Cyrill, O.S.B., J.C.D., Judicial Procedure in Dismissal of Clerical Exempt Religious, 107 pp., 1923.
20. Dargin, Rev. Edward Vincent, S.T.B., J.C.D., Reserved Cases According to the Code of Canon Law, IV-103 pp., 1924.
21. Godfrey, Rev. John A., S.T.B., J.C.D., The Right of Patronage According to the Code of Canon Law, 153 pp., 1924.
22. Hagedorn, Rev. Francis Edward, J.C.D., General Legislation on Indulgences, II-154 pp., 1924.
23. King, Rev. James Ignatius, J.C.D., The Administration of the Sacraments to Dying Non-Catholics, V-141 pp., 1924.
24. Winslow, Rev. Francis Joseph, O.F.M., J.C.D., Vicars and Prefects Apostolic, IV-149 pp., 1924.
25. Correa, Rev. Jose Servelion, S.T.L., J.C.D., La Potestad Legislativa de la Iglesia Catolica, IV-127 pp., 1925.
26. Dugan, Rev. Henry Francis, A.M., J.C.D., The Judiciary Department of the Diocesan Curia, 87 pp., 1925.
27. Keller, Rev. Charles Frederick, S.T.B., J.C.D., Mass Stipends, 167 pp., 1925.
28. Paschang, Rev. John Linus, J.C.D., The Sacramentals According to the Code of Canon Law, 129 pp., 1925.
29. Piontek, Rev. Cyrillus, O.F.M., S.T.B., J.C.D., De Indulto Exclaustrationis necnon Saecularizationis, XIII-289 pp., 1925.
30. Kearney, Rev. Richard Joseph, S.T.B., J.C.D., Sponsors at Baptism According to the Code of Canon Law, IV-127 pp., 1925.
31. Bartlett, Rev. Chester Joseph, A.M., LL.B., J.C.D., The Tenure of Parochial Property in the United States of America, V-108 pp., 1926.
32. Kilker, Rev. Adrian Jerome, J.C.D., Extreme Unction, V-425 pp., 1926.
33. McCormick, Rev. Robert Emmett, J.C.D., Confessors of Religious, VIII-266 pp., 1926.
34. Miller, Rev. Newton Thomas, J.C.D., Founded Masses According to the Code of Canon Law, VII-93 pp., 1926.
35. Roelker, Rev. Edward G., S.T.D., J.C.D., Principles of Privilege According to the Code of Canon Law, XI-166 pp., 1926.
36. Bakalarczyk, Rev. Richardus, M.I.C., J.U.D., De Novitiatu, VIII-208 pp., 1927.
37. Pizzuti, Rev. Lawrence, O.F.M., J.U.L., De Parochis Religiosis, 1927. (Not Printed.)
38. Bliley, Rev. Nicholas Martin, O.S.B., J.C.D., Altars According to the Code of Canon Law, XIX-132 pp., 1927.
39. Brown, Mr. Brendan Francis, A.B., LL.M., J.U.D., The Canonical Juristic Personality with Special Reference to its Status in the United States of America, V-212 pp., 1927.
40. Cavanaugh, Rev. William Thomas, C.P., J.U.D., The Reservation of the Blessed Sacrament, VIII-101 pp., 1927.

41. Doheny, Rev. William J., C.S.C., A.B., J.U.D., Church Property: Modes of Acquisition, X-118 pp., 1927.
42. Feldhaus, Rev. Aloysius H., C.PP.S., J.C.D., Oratories, IX-141 pp., 1927.
43. Kelly, Rev. James Patrick, A.B., J.C.D., The Jurisdiction of the Simple Confessor, X-208 pp., 1927.
44. Neuberger, Rev. Nicholas J., J.C.D., Canon 6 or the Relation of the Codex Juris Canonici to the Preceding Legislation, V-95 pp., 1927.
45. O'Keefe, Rev. Gerald Michael, J.C.D., Matrimonial Dispensations, Powers of Bishops, Priests, and Confessors, VIII-232 pp., 1927.
46. Quigley, Rev. Joseph A. M., A.B., J.C.D., Condemned Societies, 139 pp., 1927.
47. Zaplotnik, Rev. Johannes Leo, J.C.D., De Vicariis Foraneis, X-142 pp., 1927.
48. Duskie, Rev. John Aloysius, A.B., J.C.D., The Canonical Status of the Orientals in the United States, VIII-196 pp., 1928.
49. Hyland, Rev. Francis Edward, J.C.D., Excommunication, Its Nature, Historical Development and Effects, VIII-181 pp., 1928.
50. Reinmann, Rev. Gerald Joseph, O.M.C., J.C.D., The Third Order Secular of Saint Francis, 201 pp., 1928.
51. Schenk, Rev. Francis J., J.C.D., The Matrimonial Impediments of Mixed Religion and Disparity of Cult, XVI-318 pp., 1929.
52. Coady, Rev. John Joseph, S.T.D., J.U.D., A.M., The Appointment of Pastors, VIII-150 pp., 1929.
53. Kay, Rev. Thomas Henry, J.C.D., Competence in Matrimonial Procedure, VIII-164 pp., 1929.
54. Turner, Rev. Sidney Joseph, C.P., J.U.D., The Vow of Poverty, XLIX-217 pp., 1929.
55. Kearney, Rev. Raymond A., A.B., S.T.D., J.C.D., The Principles of Delegation, VII-149 pp., 1929.
56. Conran, Rev. Edward James, A.B., J.C.D., The Interdict,, V-163 pp., 1930.
57. O'Neill, Rev. William H., J.C.D., Papal Rescripts of Favor, VII-218 pp., 1930.
58. Bastnagel, Rev. Clement Vincent, J.U.D., The Appointment of Parochial Adjutants and Assistants, XV-257 pp., 1930.
59. Ferry, Rev. William A., A.B., J.C.D., Stole Fees, V-136 pp., 1930.
60. Costello, Rev. John Michael, A.B., J.C.D., Domicile and Quasi-Domicile, VII-201 pp., 1930.
61. Kremer, Rev. Michael Nicholas, A.B., S.T.B., J.C.D., Church Support in the United States, VI-136 pp., 1930.
62. Angulo, Rev. Luis, C.M., J.C.D., Legislation de la Iglesia sobre la intencion en la application de la Santa Misa, VII-104 pp., 1931.
63. Frey, Rev. Wolfgang Norbert, O.S.B., A.B., J.C.D., The Act of Religious Profession, VIII-174 pp., 1931.

64. Roberts, Rev. James Brendan, A.B., J.C.D., The Banns of Marriage, XIV-140 pp., 1931.
65. Ryder, Rev. Raymond Aloysius, A.B., J.C.D., Simony, IX-151 pp., 1931.
66. Campagna, Rev. Angelo, Ph.D., J.U.D., Il Vicario Generale del Vescovo, VII-205 pp., 1931.
67. Cox, Rev. Joseph Godfrey, A.B., J.C.D., The Administration of Seminaries, VI-124 pp., 1931.
68. Gregory, Rev. Donald J., J.U.D., The Pauline Privilege, XV-165 pp., 1931.
69. Donohue, Rev. John F., J.C.D., The Impediment of Crime, VII-110 pp., 1931.
70. Dooley, Rev. Eugene A., O.M.I., J.C.D., Church Law on Sacred Relics, IX-143 pp., 1931.
71. Orth, Rev. Clement Raymond, O.M.C., J.C.D., The Approbation of Religious Institutes, 171 pp., 1931.
72. Pernicone, Rev. Joseph M., A.B., J.C.D., The Ecclesiastical Prohibition of Books, XII-267 pp., 1932.
73. Clinton, Rev. Connell, A.B., J.C.D., The Paschal Precept, IX-108 pp., 1932.
74. Donnelly, Rev. Francis B., A.M., S.T.L., J.C.D., The Diocesan Synod, VIII-125 pp., 1932.
75. Torrente, Rev. Camilo, C.M.F., J.C.D., Las Procesiones Sagradas, V-145 pp., 1932.
76. Murphy, Rev. Edwin J., C.PP.S., J.C.D., Suspension Ex Informata Conscientia, XI-122 pp., 1932.
77. MacKenzie, Rev. Eric F., A.M., S.T.L., J.C.D., The Delict of Heresy in its Commission, Penalization, Absolution, VII-124 pp., 1932.
78. Lyons, Rev. Avitus E., S.T.B., J.C.D., The Collegiate Tribunal of First Instance, XI-147 pp., 1932.
79. Connolly, Rev. Thomas A., J.C.D., Appeals, XI-195 pp., 1932.
80. Sangmeister, Rev. Joseph V., A.B., J.C.D., Force and Fear as Precluding Matrimonial Consent, V-211 pp., 1932.
81. Jaeger, Rev. Leo A., A.B., J.C.D., The Administration of Vacant and Quasi-Vacant Episcopal Sees in the United States, IX-229 pp., 1932.
82. Rimlinger, Rev. Herbert T., J.C.D., Error Invalidating Matrimonial Consent, VII-79 pp., 1932.
83. Barrett, Rev. John D. M., S.S., J.C.D., A Comparative Study of the Third Plenary Council of Baltimore and the Code, IX-221 pp., 1932.
84. Carberry, Rev. John J., Ph.D., S.T.D., J.C.D., The Juridical Form of Marriage, X-177 pp., 1934.
85. Dolan, Rev. John L., A.B., J.C.D., The Defensor Vinculi, XII-157 pp., 1934.
86. Hannan, Rev. Jerome D., A.M., S.T.D., LL.B., J.C.D., The Canon Law of Wills, IX-517 pp., 1934.

87. LEMIEUX, REV. DELISE A., A.M., J.C.D., The Sentence in Ecclesiastical Procedure, IX-131 pp., 1934.
88. O'ROURKE, REV. JAMES J., A.B., J.C.D., Parish Registers, VII-109 pp., 1934.
89. TIMLIN, REV. BARTHOLOMEW, O.F.M., A.M., J.C.D., Conditional Matrimonial Consent, X-381 pp., 1934.
90. WAHL, REV. FRANCIS X., A.B., J.C.D., The Matrimonial Impediments of Consanguinity and Affinity, VI-125 pp., 1934.
91. WHITE, REV. ROBERT J., A.B., LL.B., S.T.B., J.C.D., Canonical Ante-Nuptial Promises and the Civil Law, VI-152 pp., 1934.
92. HERRERA, REV. ANTONIO PARRA, O.C.D., J.C.D., Legislacion Ecclesiastica sobra el Ayuno y la Abstinencia, XI-191 pp., 1935.
93. KENNEDY, REV. EDWIN J., J.C.D., The Special Matrimonial Process in Cases of Evident Nullity, X-165 pp., 1935.
94. MANNING, REV. JOHN J., A.B., J.C.D., Presumption of Law in Matrimonial Procedure, XI-111 pp., 1935.
95. MOEDER, REV. JOHN M., J.C.D., The Proper Bishop for Ordination and Dimissorial Letters, VII-135 pp., 1935.
96. O'MARA, REV. WILLIAM A., A.B., J.C.D., Canonical Causes for Matrimonial Dispensations, IX-155 pp., 1935.
97. REILLY, REV. PETER, J.C.D., Residence of Pastors, IX-81 pp., 1935.
98. SMITH, REV. MARINER T., O.P., S.T.Lr., J.C.D., The Penal Law for Religious, VIII-169 pp., 1935.
99. WHALEN, REV. DONALD W., A.M., J.C.D., The Value of Testimonial Evidence in Matrimonial Procedure, XIII-297 pp., 1935.
100. CLEARY, REV. JOSEPH F., J.C.D., Canonical Limitations on the Alienation of Church Property, VIII-141 pp., 1936.
101. GLYNN, REV. JOHN C., J.C.D., The Promoter of Justice, XX-337 pp., 1936.
102. BRENNAN, REV. JAMES H., S.S., M.A., S.T.B., J.C.D., The Simple Convalidation of Marriage, VI-135 pp., 1937.
103. BRUNINI, REV. JOSEPH BERNARD, J.C.D., The Clerical Obligations of Canons 139 and 142, X-121 pp., 137.
104. CONNOR, REV. MAURICE, A.B., J.C.D., The Administrative Removal of Pastors, VIII-159 pp., 1937.
105. GUILFOYLE, REV. MERLIN JOSEPH, J.C.D., Custom, XI-144 pp., 1937.
106. HUGHES, REV. JAMES AUSTIN, A.B., A.M., J.C.D., Witnesses in Criminal Trials of Clerics, IX-140 pp., 1937.
107. JANSEN, REV. RAYMOND J., A.B., S.T.L., J.C.D., Canonical Provisions for Catechetical Instruction, VII-153 pp., 1937.
108. KEALY, REV. JOHN JAMES, A.B., J.C.D., The Introductory Libellus in Church Court Procedure, XI-121 pp., 1937.
109. McMANUS, REV. JAMES EDWARD, C.SS.R., J.C.D., The Administration of Temporal Goods in Religious Institutes, XVI-196 pp., 1937.

110. Moriarty, Rev. Eugene James, J.C.D., Oaths in Ecclesiastical Courts, X-115 pp., 1937.

111. Rainier, Rev. Eligius George, C.SS.R., J.C.D., Suspension of Clerics, XVII-249 pp., 1937.

112. Reilly, Rev. Thomas F., C.SS.R., J.C.D., Visitation of Religious, VI-195 pp., 1938.

113. Moriarty, Rev. Francis E., C.SS.R., J.C.D., The Extraordinary Absolution from Censures, XV-334 pp., 1938.

114. Connolly, Rev. Nicholas P., J.C.D., The Canonical Erection of Parishes, X-132 pp., 1938.

115. Donovan, Rev. James Joseph, J.C.D., The Pastor's Obligation in Prenuptial Investigation, XII-322 pp., 1938.

116. Harrigan, Rev. Robert J., M.A., S.T.B., J.C.D., The Radical Sanation of Invalid Marriages, VIII-208 pp., 1938.

117. Boffa, Rev. Conrad Humbert, J.C.D., Canonical Provisions for Catholic Schools, VII-211 pp., 1939.

118. Parsons, Rev. Anscar John, O.M.Cap., J.C.D., Canonical Elections, XII-236 pp., 1939.

119. Reilly, Rev. Edward Michael, A.B., J.C.D., The General Norms of Dispensation, XII-156 pp., 1939.

120. Ryan, Rev. Gerald Aloysius, A.B., J.C.D., Principles of Episcopal Jurisdiction, XII-172 pp., 1939.

121. Burton, Rev. Francis James, C.S.C., A.B., J.C.D., A Commentary on Canon 1125, X-222 pp., 1940.

122. Miaskiewicz, Rev. Francis Sigismund, J.C.D., Supplied Jurisdiction According to Canon 209, XII-340 pp., 1940.

123. Rice, Rev. Patrick William, A.B., J.C.D., Proof of Death in Prenuptial Investigation, VIII-156 pp., 1940.

124. Anglin, Rev. Thomas Francis, M.S., J.C.D., The Eucharistic Fast, VIII-183 pp., 1941.

125. Coleman, Rev. John Jerome, J.C.D., The Minister of Confirmation, VI-153 pp., 1941.

126. Downs, Rev. Joseph Emmanuel, A.B., J.C.D., The Concept of Clerical Immunity, XI-163 pp., 1941.

127. Esswein, Rev. Anthony Albert, J.C.D., Extrajudicial Penal Powers of Ecclesiastical Superiors, X-144 pp., 1941.

128. Farrell, Rev. Benjamin Francis, M.A., S.T.L., J.C.D., The Rights and Duties of the Local Ordinary Regarding Congregations of Women Religious of Pontifical Approval, V-195 pp., 1941.

129. Feeney, Rev. Thomas John, A.B., S.T.L., J.C.D., Restitutio in Integrum, VI-169 pp., 1941.

130. Findlay, Rev. Stephen William, O.S.B., A.B., J.C.D., Canonical Norms Governing the Deposition and Degradation of Clerics, XVII-279 pp., 1941.

131. Goodwine, Rev. John, A.B., S.T.L., J.C.D., The Right of the Church to Acquire Property, VIII-119 pp., 1941.
132. Heston, Rev. Edward Louis, C.S.C., Ph.D., S.T.D., J.C.D., The Alienation of Church Property in the United States, XII-222 pp., 1941.
133. Hogan, Rev. James John, A.B., S.T.L., J.C.D., Judicial Advocates and Procurators, XIII-200 pp., 1941.
134. Kealy, Rev. Thomas M., A.B., Litt.B., J.C.D., Dowry of Women Religious, IX-152 pp., 1941.
135. Keene, Rev. Michael James, O.S.B., J.C.D., Religious Ordinaries and Canon 198, V-164 pp., 1942.
136. Kerin, Rev. Charles A., S.S., M.A., S.T.B., J.C.D., The Privation of Christian Burial, XVI-279 pp., 1941.
137. Louis, Rev. William Francis, M.A., J.C.D., Diocesan Archives, X-101 pp., 1941.
138. McDevitt, Rev. Gilbert Joseph, A.B., J.C.D., Legitimacy and Legitimation, X-247 pp., 1941.
139. McDonough, Rev. Thomas Joseph, A.B., J.C.D., Apostolic Administrators, X-217 pp., 1941.
140. Meier, Rev. Carl Anthony, A.B., J.C.D., Penal Administrative Procedure Against Negligent Pastors, XI-240 pp., 1941.
141. Schmidt, Rev. John Rogg, A.B., J.C.D., The Principles of Authentic Interpretation in Canon 17 of the Code of Canon Law, XII-331 pp., 1941.
142. Slafkosky, Rev. Andrew Leonard, A.B., J.C.D., The Canonical Episcopal Visitation of the Diocese, X-197 pp., 1941.
143. Swoboda, Rev. Innocent Robert, O.F.M., J.C.D., Ignorance in Relation to the Imputability of Delicts, IX-271 pp., 1941.
144. Dubé, Rev. Arthur Joseph, A.B., J.C.D., The General Principles for the Reckoning of Time in Canon Law, VIII-299 pp., 1941.
145. McBride, Rev. James T., A.B., J.C.D., Incardination and Excardination of Seculars, XX-585 pp., 1941.
146. Król, Rev. John T., J.C.D., The Defendant in Ecclesiastical Trials, XII-207 pp., 1942.
147. Comyns, Rev. Joseph J., C.SS.R., A.B., J.C.D., Papal and Episcopal Administration of Church Property, XIV-155 pp., 1942.
148. Barry, Rev. Garrett Francis, O.M.I., J.C.D., Violation of the Cloister, XII-260 pp., 1942.
149. Bolduc, Rev. Gatien, C.S.V., A.B., S.T.L., J.C.D., Les Études dans les Religions Cléricales, VIII-155 pp., 1942.
150. Boyle, Rev. David John, M.A., J.C.D., The Juridic Effects of Moral Certitude on Pre-Nuptial Guarantees, XII-188 pp., 1942.
151. Canavan, Rev. Walter Joseph, M.A., Litt.D., J.C.D., The Profession of Faith, XII-143 pp., 1942.
152. Desrochers, Rev. Bruno, A.B., Ph.L., S.T.B., J.C.D., Le Premier Concile Plénier de Québec et le Code de Droit Canonique, XIV-186 pp., 1942.

153. Dillon, Rev. Robert Edward, A.B., J.C.D., Common Law Marriage, X-148 pp., 1942.
154. Dodwell, Rev. Edward John, Ph.D., S.T.B., J.C.L., The Time and Place for the Celebration of Marriage.
155. Donnellan, Rev. Thomas Andrew, A.B., J.C.D., The Obligation of the Missa pro Populo, VII-131 pp., 1942.
156. Eltz, Rev. Louis Anthony, A.B., J.C.L., Cooperation in Crime.
157. Gass, Rev. Sylvester Francis, M.A., J.C.D., Ecclesiastical Pensions, XI-206 pp., 1942.
158. Guiniven, Rev. John Joseph, C.SS.R., J.C.D., The Precept of Hearing Mass, XIV-188 pp., 1942.
159. Gulczynski, Rev. John Theophilus, J.C.D., The Desecration and Violation of Churches.
160. Hammill, Rev. John Leo, M.A., J.C.D., The Obligations of the Traveler According to Canon 14, VIII-204 pp., 1942.
161. Haydt, Rev. John Joseph, A.B., J.C.D., Reserved Benefices, XI-148 pp., 1942.
162. Huser, Rev. Roger John, O.F.M., A.B., J.C.D., The Crime of Abortion in Canon Law.
163. Kearney, Rev. Francis Patrick, A.B., S.T.L., J.C.L., The Principles of Canon 1127.
164. Linahen, Rev. Leo James, S.T.L., J.C.D., De Absolutione Complicis In Peccato Turpi, 114 pp., 1942.
165. McCloskey, Rev. Joseph Aloysius, A.B., J.C.D., The Subject of Ecclesiastical Law According to Canon 12, XVII-246 pp., 1942.
166. O'Neill, Rev. Francis Joseph, C.SS.R., J.C.D., The Dismissal of Religious in Temporary Vows, XIII-220 pp., 1942.
167. Prince, Rev. John Edward, A.B., S.T.B., J.C.D., The Diocesan Chancellor, X-136 pp., 1942.
168. Riesner, Rev. Albert Joseph, C.SS.R., J.C.D., Apostates and Fugitives from Religious Institutes, IX-168 pp., 1942.
169. Stenger, Rev. Joseph Bernard, J.C.D., The Mortgaging of Church Property, 186 pp., 1942.
170. Waldron, Rev. Joseph Francis, A.B., J.C.D., The Minister of Baptism, XII-197 pp., 1942.
171. Willett, Rev. Robert Albert, J.C.D., The Probative Value of Documents in Ecclesiastical Trials, X-124 pp., 1942.
172. Woeber, Rev. Edward Martin, M.A., J.C.D., The Interpellations, XII-161 pp., 1942.
173. Benko, Rev. Matthew Aloysius, O.S.B.. M.A., J.C.L., The Abbot *Nullius*.
174. Christ, Rev. Joseph James, M.A., S.T.L., J.C.L., Dispensation from Vindicative Penalties.
175. Clancy, Rev. Patrick M. J., O.P., A.B., S.T.Lr., J.C.L., The Local Religious Superior.

176. Clarke, Rev. Thomas James, J.C.L., Parish Societies.
177. Connolly, Rev. John Patrick, S.T.L., J.C.L., Synodal Examiners and Parish Priest Consultors.
178. Drumm, Rev. William Martin, A.B., J.C.L., Hospital Chaplains.
179. Flanagan, Rev. Bernard Joseph, A.B., S.T.L., J.C.L., The Canonical Erection of Religious Houses.
180. Kelleher, Rev. Stephen Joseph, A.B., S.T.B., J.C.L., Discussions with Non-Catholics: Canonical Legislation.
181. Lewis, Rev. Gordian, C.P., J.C.L., Chapters in Religious Institutes.
182. Marx, Rev. Adolph, J.C.L., The Declaration of Nullity of Marriages Contracted Outside the Church.
183. Matulenas, Rev. Raymond Anthony, O.S.B., A.B., J.C.L., Communication, a Source of Privileges.
184. O'Leary, Rev. Charles Gerard, C.SS.R., Religious Dismissed After Perpetual Profession.
185. Power, Rev. Cornelius Michael, J.C.L., The Blessing of Cemeteries.
186. Shuhler, Rev. Ralph Vincent, O.S.A., J.C.L., Privileges of Religious to Absolve and Dispense.
187. Ziolkowski, Rev. Thaddeus Stanislaus, A.B., J.C.L., The Consecration and Blessing of Churches.

www.ingramcontent.com/pod-product-compliance
Lightning Source LLC
LaVergne TN
LVHW050224080826
844660LV00012B/466

* 9 7 8 0 8 1 3 2 2 3 7 6 6 *